I HATE HAMLET

BY PAUL RUDNICK

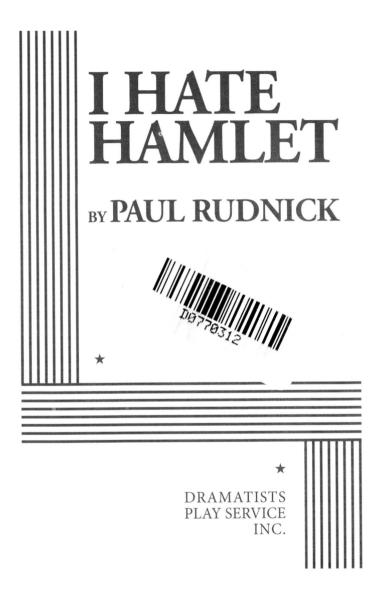

★

DRAMATISTS
PLAY SERVICE
INC.

I HATE HAMLET was originally produced at the Walter Kerr Theatre (Jujamcyn Theaters, James B. Freydberg, Robert G. Perkins and Margo Lion, Producers), in New York City, on April 8, 1991. It was directed by Michael Engler; the set design was by Tony Straiges; the costume design was by Jane Greenwood; the lighting design was by Paul Gallo; the sound design was by Scott Lehrer; fight direction was by B.H. Barry and the original music was by Kim Sherman. The cast was as follows:

FELICIA DANTINE .... Caroline Aaron
ANDREW RALLY .... Evan Handler
DEIRDRE MCDAVEY .... Jane Adams
LILLIAN TROY .... Celeste Holm
JOHN BARRYMORE .... Nicol Williamson
GARY PETER LEFKOWITZ .... Adam Arkin

I HATE HAMLET
Copyright © 1992, Paul Rudnick

All Rights Reserved

NOTE ON BILLING

Anyone receiving permission to produce I HATE HAMLET is required to give credit to the Author as sole and exclusive Author of the Play on the title page of all programs distributed in connection with performances of the Play and in all instances in which the title of the Play appears, including printed or digital materials for advertising, publicizing or otherwise exploiting the Play and/or a production thereof. The name of the Author must appear on a separate line, in which no other name appears, immediately beneath the title and in size of type equal to 50% of the size of the largest, most prominent letter used for the title of the Play. No person, firm or entity may receive credit larger or more prominent than that accorded the Author. The following acknowledgment must appear on the title page of all programs distributed in connection with performances of the Play:

Originally produced by Jujamcyn Theatres,
James B. Freydberg, Robert G. Perkins, Margo Lion.
Original production directed by Michael Engler.

SPECIAL NOTE ON MUSIC

A CD with cue sheet containing the original music composed by Kim Sherman for this play is available through the Play Service for $35.00, plus shipping and handling. The nonprofessional fee for the use of this music is $15.00 per performance.

SPECIAL NOTE ON SONGS/RECORDINGS

Dramatists Play Service neither holds the rights to nor grants permission to use any songs or recordings mentioned in the Play. Permission for performances of copyrighted songs, arrangements or recordings mentioned in this Play is not included in our license agreement. The permission of the copyright owner(s) must be obtained for any such use. For any songs and/or recordings mentioned in the Play, other songs, arrangements, or recordings may be substituted provided permission from the copyright owner(s) of such songs, arrangements or recordings is obtained; or songs, arrangements or recordings in the public domain may be substituted.

For Helen Merrill

CHARACTERS
(in order of appearance)

Felicia Dantine
Andrew Rally
Deirdre McDavey
Lillian Troy
John Barrymore
Gary Peter Lefkowitz

I HATE HAMLET
Notes on Production

I Hate Hamlet was inspired by circumstances: a few years back, I answered an ad in the New York *Times* real estate section, for a "medieval duplex." The apartment had been occupied by John Barrymore in 1917, and he had renovated the premises into a Gothic retreat which he titled "The Alchemist's Corner." More detailed information on both Barrymore and the apartment can be found in any number of Barrymore biographies, including Gene Fowler's *Good Night, Sweet Prince* and Margot Peters' more recent *The House of Barrymore.*

The play itself is, above all, a tribute to actors. All roles should be played with a maximum of comic verve. Barrymore was a witty and rakish fellow; the role should be informed with a wicked, bounding glee, and absolutely no hint of pedantry. Andrew Rally should possess his own potent charm, as both he and Barrymore are stars.

Gary Peter Lefkowitz must never become an easy villain, for while he is crass and calculating, he is never stupid. He should be played with a shameless exuberance. Gary loves his life. *I Hate Hamlet* deals with all our secret, dirty thoughts concerning high art; we've all dozed through our share of Shakespeare. Gary embodies these wayward, honest impulses, and the audience should find him both appalling and irresistible.

Deirdre McDavey must also be played with delicious comic fervor, as she is not a ninny, but a wild romantic. She enjoys a whole-hearted swoon every few seconds, and she is delightfully resilient. She is not a mere kook, but a beacon of breathless wonder. Felicia Dantine and Lillian Troy are equally strong figures; everyone in the play takes a lusty pleasure in their own personality. Lillian, in Act One, should be played with a wry toughness, a no-nonsense quality; in this manner, her moonlit love scene in Act Two can come as more of a surprise, and a scene of real emotion.

The play should be performed with speed and gusto, as an unashamed boulevard comedy. Like any comic work, it demands absolute precision. The duel which ends Act One and the lesson in curtain calls which concludes Act Two require practiced choreography, so that the result in performance can appear effortless. Music may be employed throughout the play, and is particularly effective for Barrymore's entrance, the duel and Lillian's waltz. A tape of the Broadway score, composed by the invaluable Kim Sherman, is available through the Play Service.

The play is a ghost story, so magical effects are always appropriate. The apartment is an enchanted locale, and this should be reflected in the set, lighting and costume design; on Broadway, the work of designers Tony Straiges, Jane Greenwood and Paul Gallo lent the play a luscious jewel-box quality. That production's gifted director, Michael Engler, who also directed an earlier workshop of the play, was instrumental in setting a tone of stylish deviltry. *I Hate Hamlet* celebrates the theater, in all its artifice and happy dementia. May the Barrymore panache rule all productions.

– Paul Rudnick

I HATE HAMLET

ACT ONE

Scene 1

Time: The present.

Place: The top floor apartment of a brownstone just off Washington Square in New York City. The apartment's architecture is highly theatrical, a gothic melange of oak beams, plank floors and plaster work designed to resemble roughhewn stone. There is a deep window seat stage left, with treetops visible through a leaded bay window. Upstage right is the front door to the apartment, and an open archway reveals a hall, presumably leading to a kitchen and bedrooms. Center stage is a grand marble fireplace, as regal and gargoyled as possible. Beside the fireplace stands an elaborately carved wooden stairway, which curves first to a landing and then up a short flight to an impressive, rounded gothic door, which leads to the roof. The design of the apartment must be, above all, exceedingly romantic and old world, a Manhattan interpretation of a King Arthur domicile; think Hollywood/Jacobean.

At present almost all of the apartment is shrouded in dropcloths and sheets, providing an ambience of ghost-provoking mystery. The apartment's current occupant has only just moved in; cardboard cartons are stacked about, amid mounds of partially unpacked goods. The sparse furnishings are stark and modern, functional at best. There is a square-ish couch off to one side, upholstered in white canvas. Folding chairs and the stacks of cartons provide additional seating.

As the curtain rises, the stage is in darkness. Mystic music, and a supernatural lighting effect might precede the action.

The doorknob on the front door rattles, and the door is flung open. Felicia Dantine bursts into the room, and immediately bustles around the apartment, switching on lights. Felicia is a tall, imposing woman with a mane of boldly streaked hair. She wears high suede boots, and a long vest of ragged purple leather and fur. Felicia is a real estate agent, with an almost carnal passion for Manhattan apartments. She speaks in a hoarse, buoyant voice, with a hint of Queens nasality, a jubilant New York honk.

Andrew Rally, the apartment's new tenant, follows Felicia into the apartment. Andrew is an actor, in his late twenties or early thirties; he is handsome and charming, possessing the polished ease of a television star. Andrew could easily glide through life, wafting on a cloud of good looks and affability. He is not without ego, however; he is more than accustomed to being the center of attention.

This is Andrew's first moment in the apartment; he carries a box of personal belongings. He stares at his new surroundings, with a mixture of awe and uneasiness.

ANDREW. *(Looking around.)* Oh my God.
FELICIA. Isn't it fabulous? I'm so glad you took it sight unseen. I just knew it was perfect.
ANDREW. It's amazing, but ... gee, I'm sorry. This isn't what we talked about. I was thinking of, you know, something ... less.
FELICIA. But it's a landmark! John Barrymore, the legendary star! And now you, Andrew Rally, from *LA Medical!* I loved that show! You were adorable! Why did they cancel it?
ANDREW. Bad time slot, shaky network — I don't think I

can live here, this isn't what we discussed.

FELICIA. I know, I know — but honey, I'm not just a broker. I want you to be happy! You belong here.

ANDREW. Don't worry, it's my mistake, I'll move back to my hotel, it's fine.

FELICIA. *(Gesturing to the cartons.)* But your things are here! It's a match! You and Barrymore!

ANDREW. *(Flattered.)* Please, I'm no Barrymore.

FELICIA. Of course you are, Dr. Jim Corman, rookie surgeon! I even love those commercials you do! What is it — Tomboy Chocolate?

ANDREW. Trailburst Nuggets. It's a breakfast cereal.

FELICIA. *(Delighted.)* And...?

ANDREW and FELICIA. *(Singing the jingle.)* "An anytime snack!" *(The doorbell buzzes.)*

FELICIA. An anytime snack! I love it! I love that ad! *(Felicia goes to the intercom, which is located in a niche beside the front door. Into the intercom.)* Hello? He sure is! *(Passing the receiver to Andrew.)* For you! Your first guest!

ANDREW. *(Into the receiver.)* Hello? Sure ... come on up. Please! *(To Felicia.)* It's my girlfriend. She can't wait to see the place.

FELICIA. *(Excited.)* Do I know her? Was she on your show?

ANDREW. No, I met Deirdre in New York. But I'm from LA. I like modern things. High tech. Look at this place — I mean, is there a moat? *(There is a knock on the front door. Andrew opens it. Deirdre McDavey is standing outside, clutching a bouquet of roses. Deirdre wears a green wool cape, a long challis skirt, a lacy antique blouse and pointy, lace-up Victorian boots. Her hair streams down her back, Alice-in-Wonderland style. Deirdre is Andrew's girlfriend; she is twenty-nine years old, but appears much younger. Deirdre is the breathless soul of romantic enthusiasm. She is always on the verge of a swoon; to Deirdre, life is a miracle a minute. Deirdre is irresistibly appealing, a Valley girl imagining herself a Brontë heroine. Deirdre stands in the doorway, trembling and on the verge of tears. Her eyes are clenched shut. She is practically hyperventilating; she speaks in a passionate, strangled whisper.)*

DEIRDRE. Andrew...?

ANDREW. *(With amused patience.)* Yes, Deirdre?

DEIRDRE. Andrew ... am I ... here?

ANDREW. This is it. *(Deirdre steps into the apartment and opens her eyes. She gasps. As she tours the premises she removes her cape and hands Andrew the roses and her velvet shoulderbag.)*

DEIRDRE. Oh, *Andrew* ... his walls ... his floor ... the staircase to his roof ... the air he breathed ... oh Andrew, just being here makes you a part of history!

FELICIA. And I'm the broker!

DEIRDRE. *(To Felicia.)* I worship you! *(The doorbell buzzes again.)*

ANDREW. I'll get it.

FELICIA. *(Handing Deirdre her business card.)* Hi. Felicia Dantine.

ANDREW. *(Into the intercom receiver.)* Hello? Come on up.

FELICIA. Isn't this place amazing? The Barrymore thing? The morning it comes on the market, I get Andrew's call.

DEIRDRE. *(Impressed.) No.*

FELICIA. Two famous actors! It's freaky. Are you in the business? *(There is a knock on the door. Andrew opens the door; Lillian Troy is outside. Lillian is a striking, silver-haired woman in her seventies; she wears an elegant mink coat over a simple navy dress, and carries a bottle of champagne. She is smoking an unfiltered Camel cigarette. Lillian speaks with a regal German accent, and has a no-nonsense manner, combined with a delight at any sort of high-jinks. Lillian is Andrew's agent. As the door opens, Lillian is coughing, a real smoker's hack.)*

ANDREW. Lillian, Lillian, are you okay?

LILLIAN. *(Finishing her coughing.)* I am fine. *(Passing Andrew the champagne.)* Take it. *(Surveying the premises.)* This is it. As I remember.

ANDREW. What?

LILLIAN. I have been here before. But I had to be certain. *(As Deirdre curtsies.)* Deirdre, you I know. *(To Felicia.)* Hello. I am Lillian Troy. I am Andrew's agent. The scum of the earth.

FELICIA. Hi. Felicia Dantine. Real estate. I win.

ANDREW. *(To Lillian.)* What do you mean, you've been here before?

LILLIAN.   It was in, oh, the forties I imagine. I had just come to America. *(Looking around.)* It was magical. This great window. The cottage on the roof. Fresh flowers everywhere. I had a little fling. Andrew, perhaps you have found my hairpins.

ANDREW.   Lillian — you had a fling here?

FELICIA.   In this apartment?

DEIRDRE.   With who?

LILLIAN.   Whom do you think?

ANDREW.   Barrymore?

DEIRDRE.   *(Awestruck.)* Lillian — you and ... Barrymore?

FELICIA.   Here?

LILLIAN.   I am an old lady. The elderly should not discuss romance, it is distasteful. And creates jealousy. And Andrew has such marvelous news — does everyone know?

DEIRDRE.   What? What news?

ANDREW.   I haven't told because ... I'm not sure how I feel about it.

DEIRDRE.   What? Andrew, what haven't you told me?

ANDREW.   Well ... you know Shakespeare in the Park, right? The open-air theater, by the lake?

FELICIA.   I went once. It poured. Right on Coriolanus. Didn't help. They kept going.

DEIRDRE.   *(To Andrew.)* What? Tell us!

ANDREW.   Well, this summer they're doing *All's Well*, and ... another one.

DEIRDRE.   Which one?

ANDREW.   *(Taking a deep breath.)* Hamlet.

DEIRDRE.   Oh my God. Wait. Laertes?

ANDREW.   Hamlet.

DEIRDRE.   The *lead?*

ANDREW.   Yeah, Hamlet.

LILLIAN.   Ya! Isn't that extraordinary? *(Deirdre is starting to hyperventilate again. She holds up her hands, and backs away from Andrew.)*

DEIRDRE.   You ... are ... playing ... Hamlet? My boyfriend is playing Hamlet?

ANDREW.   I don't know why they cast me.

LILLIAN.   Because you are talented. You auditioned five times. They saw something.

FELICIA.   Dr. Jim Corman! You'll pack the place! I'll even come. Is it the real *Hamlet*? Or like, a musical?

ANDREW.   The real one. And she's right, of course, I'm sure they only asked me because of the TV show. I'm a gimmick. I don't know why I said yes.

LILLIAN.   Schnookie — we are talking about *Hamlet*.

DEIRDRE.   Wouldn't it be great if we could like, go back in time and tell Barrymore?

FELICIA.   Why?

DEIRDRE.   I mean, he was the greatest Hamlet of all time — isn't that what people say?

LILLIAN.   That is true. And Andrew, you know — he lived here for many years. Perhaps when he played Hamlet.

DEIRDRE.   And now you're here — I bet this is all happening for a reason.

FELICIA.   'Cause you were cancelled! *(Looking around, sniffing the air.)* I get this feeling sometimes, in special apartments. About the people who lived there. *(Felicia climbs the staircase to the first landing. She raises her arms. Intoning.)* Barrymore. Barrymore! *(In the distance, a bell tolls, from a belltower. Everyone looks up.)*

LILLIAN.   What was that?

FELICIA.   The church, down the street. The clock in the belltower.

ANDREW.   But ... it's six o'clock. It only struck once.

DEIRDRE.   Oh my God. Just like in *Hamlet*. Right before the ghost of Hamlet's father appears. He comes when the clock strikes one.

FELICIA.   Which means...?

ANDREW.   That we live in New York. Where everything's broken.

DEIRDRE.   But what if it's an omen?

FELICIA.   Right. Barrymore. Hamlet. The connection. Maybe he's trying to contact us.

ANDREW.   *(Pointing to the messy batch of menus which have been slipped under the front door.)* Yeah. Maybe he's the one who's

14

been slipping all these take-out menus under the door.

DEIRDRE. Andrew!

FELICIA. *(Still on the landing.)* Don't joke. Maybe he's ... around. It's possible. Totally.

DEIRDRE. Oh my God. What if we could reach out to him, across time and space? Wouldn't that be a great idea?

LILLIAN. Don't ask me about great ideas. I am German.

FELICIA. *(Coming down the stairs.)* Wait. Guys. You know — I'm psychic.

DEIRDRE. Oh my God!

LILLIAN. What do you mean?

FELICIA. I've made contact. With the other side. I go into this pre-conscious state, like a trance. And I speak to a spirit guide.

ANDREW. A spirit guide?

FELICIA. Yeah — my Mom. We were real close. After she died, I went into such a slump. I tried everything, therapy, encounter groups, you name it. Finally I saw this ad, for a course — "Spiritual Transcommunication: Beyond The Physical Sphere."

LILLIAN. So you talk to your mother?

FELICIA. Right. Is your Mom gone too? Would you like to contact her?

LILLIAN. No. Why break a habit?

DEIRDRE. The clock. This apartment. Hamlet. This is pre-ordained. I think we should do it.

ANDREW. Do what?

DEIRDRE. Contact Barrymore. A seance. Right now. *(There is a pause, as everyone looks at each other; the women are all extremely excited at the prospect of a seance, while Andrew has his doubts.)*

FELICIA. I've never tried anyone but Ma. But I'm game!

ANDREW. I don't think so.

LILLIAN. But who can tell? Barrymore might return. As he promised me.

DEIRDRE. Lillian — were you really here? With Barrymore?

LILLIAN. Ask him yourself.

ANDREW. No, come on — this is just an apartment. It's not

magical, and there aren't any ghosts or supernatural pheno-
mena. And we're not having a seance. *(The door to the roof
creaks open, and then slams shut, all by itself.)* Do we need
candles?

FELICIA.   Candles are great. *(Andrew rummages through a box
to find a candle.)*

DEIRDRE.   Felicia, what about a table?

FELICIA.   Perfect. *(During the next few speeches, Deirdre and
Felicia move a card table to C., and set chairs or crates around it.
Lillian supervises.)*

DEIRDRE.   *(As she moves the table.)* This is just like at the
beginning of *Hamlet,* when the guards call out to the ghost.
(With gusto.)

    "Stay, illusion!

    If thou hast any sound or use of voice,

    Speak to me!"

LILLIAN.   *(Holding out her arms.)*

    "If there be any good thing to be done

    That may to thee do ease and grace to me

    Speak to me!"

DEIRDRE.   "O, speak!"

LILLIAN.   "Stay and speak!"

ANDREW.   Oh my God. Felicia, is this how you usually
operate? Seances? Shakespeare?

FELICIA.   Honey, I've been a broker for almost fifteen years.
In Greenwich Village. Try human sacrifice. And cheese. *(Sur-
veying the table.)* Okay, everybody sit. How should we do this?
I know — first I'll try and contact Ma, and then see if she can
get ahold of Barrymore. *(By this point, Deirdre, Lillian and
Felicia are all seated around the table.)*

LILLIAN.   May I smoke? Does anyone mind?

DEIRDRE.   Oh Lillian, it's such a terrible thing to do, and
we all love you so much, do you have to?

LILLIAN.   *(Sighing.)* Very well. *(She puts down her cigarette.)* You
know, I really must stop.

DEIRDRE.   Smoking?

LILLIAN.   No — asking. *(Andrew has located a candle and stuck
it in a bottle. He sets the bottle on the table.)*

FELICIA. *(To Andrew.)* Now hit the lights, okay, hon? I'm gonna enter this trance state, so Andy, think about what you want to ask Barrymore.

DEIRDRE. Has he met Shakespeare?

LILLIAN. Is it hot?

DEIRDRE. Lillian, Barrymore is not in Hell. I'm sure Felicia never even deals with people ... down there.

FELICIA. Well, if I have a legal problem ... okay everybody, put your hands on the table, palms down, it helps the flow. Now close your eyes. *(By now Andrew has dimmed the lights; the room is lit only by the candle. Andrew has joined the others seated around the table. Everyone joins hands and closes their eyes.)* Now just clear your minds, totally blank, clean slate. Deep, even breathing. *(Everyone is now breathing in unison, very deeply. Lillian coughs. Everyone continues breathing. Felicia lifts her head. A convulsion shakes Felicia's body; her head drops. As her head rises, she utters a long, guttural, effectively bizarre moan. Finally, as contact is made, Felicia's head pops up, and she assumes a cheery brightness, as if talking on the phone. Her eyes remain shut during her conversation with her mother.)* Yeah Ma, it's me ... fine, fine, you? *(Confidentially, to the group.)* I got her!... Ma, listen to me, I need your help, I'm here with Andrew Rally ... yeah, "LA Medical" ... Ma, listen, he wants to talk to someone, over there ... no Ma, he's seeing someone ... Ma, I think he's having a career crisis, he's gonna do Shakespeare, and he needs to talk to Barrymore, right, John Barrymore ... from the movies ... okay, okay — hang on ... *(To Andrew.)* She needs to know, what do you want to ask Barrymore? What's your question?

DEIRDRE. *(Thrilled.)* Andrew, ask!

ANDREW. Ask him what?

DEIRDRE. Ask him about *Hamlet!*

LILLIAN. Ask him for advice!

ANDREW. But I don't want advice, and I don't want to play Hamlet, I mean I don't think I do, I mean, I hate *Hamlet!* *(As Andrew says "I hate* Hamlet," *there is a deafening crack of thunder. A gust of wind fills the apartment, extinguishing the candle. There is a second thunderclap, and a bolt of lightning streaks across the sky. An enormous shadow is thrown across the wall, of a handsome pro-*

file. Only Andrew sees the shadow.)

LILLIAN. Andrew!

DEIRDRE. Don't say that! *(Felicia is again overtaken by a convulsion, as the astral contact is broken. She makes a wild hacking noise, as if coughing up a furball. She rocks, and leaves the table, her body spasming.)* Felicia! *(Andrew rises and runs to the lights. He flips on the switch.)*

FELICIA. What? Is he ... hold on. Yeah? What happened? Did I get her? Ma?

DEIRDRE. You talked to her, and she tried to contact Barrymore, but something happened! There was lightning!

LILLIAN. It was marvelous!

FELICIA. Did you see anything? A sign? A woman with rhinestone glasses?

DEIRDRE. I don't think so ...

ANDREW. *(Firmly.)* No. We didn't see anything. No Barrymore.

LILLIAN. As far as we know.

FELICIA. I'm sorry, you know ... Ma's really the only one I get. It's emotional, there's gotta be a real need. Andy, I'm sorry.

ANDREW. No, please, you were fine. And I'm glad about your Mom and I can't believe I even considered playing Hamlet. This is all ... not possible.

LILLIAN. Rally — do me a favor. Do not be like all the others. Everywhere I look, I am disappointed. You must have faith. Barrymore would insist.

DEIRDRE. He could still appear.

FELICIA. Sometimes you gotta bribe 'em — the spirits. You need something they really liked, when they were alive. Especially the first contact.

DEIRDRE. Really? What did your mother like? What did you use?

FELICIA. It was tough, I tried everything. Jewelry, sponge cake, finally I just said Ma, it's after ten, the rates are down. Bingo! Should we try again?

DEIRDRE. Of course!

ANDREW. No. Absolutely not. No more.

LILLIAN.   Oh Rally, where is your sense of adventure? Television has ruined you. *(The sound of thunder and rainfall is heard, increasingly heavy.)* I must go. I only wanted a look at the place.

FELICIA.   I'd better split too. Before it starts pouring.

LILLIAN.   *(Gazing around.)* It is ... as I recall. Perhaps smaller. But still a jewel. The elevator is new. *(She starts coughing.)*

ANDREW.   Lillian, are you okay? Have you been to the doctor?

LILLIAN.   *(Cutting him off.)* Doctors. I have seen too many doctors. Mostly played by you. Enough. Rally, when do rehearsals begin?

ANDREW.   I'm not discussing it.

LILLIAN.   But I need to negotiate, on your behalf. It is Shakespeare in the Park. It is non-profit. I will make them bleed. *(Felicia and Lillian now have their coats on.)*

FELICIA.   *(Taking a last look at the apartment.)* It's a great space. Don't listen to me, I say that in cabs. Someday they're gonna say, Andrew Rally lived here!

DEIRDRE.   A great Hamlet!

LILLIAN.   And an anytime snack.

ANDREW.   Out!

FELICIA.   Bye, kids!

LILLIAN.   Wait. *(Lillian pauses, feeling an emanation. She goes to the mantel, and finds an object. She gleefully holds the object aloft.)* My hairpin! *(A chord of ghostly music is heard. Felicia and Lillian exit. Andrew and Deirdre face each other, both excited at being alone together.)*

DEIRDRE.   Andrew ... *(Deirdre runs into Andrew's arms, and they embrace.)* Hamlet! Why didn't you tell me?

ANDREW.   Because I knew you would be the most excited. And I knew you would tell me I have to do it.

DEIRDRE.   Of course you have to!

ANDREW.   But why? Just because it's supposed to be this ultimate challenge? Because everyone's supposed to dream of playing Hamlet?

DEIRDRE.   No — because it's the most beautiful play ever

19

written. It's about how awful life is, and how everything gets
betrayed. But then Hamlet tries to make things better. And he
dies!

ANDREW.   Which tells us ...

DEIRDRE.   At least he tried!

ANDREW.   But why do I have to be Hamlet? I can get another show, maybe even movies. I don't need Hamlet.

DEIRDRE.   But Andrew — you went to drama school.

ANDREW.   Only for two years.

DEIRDRE.   But wasn't it wonderful? The great plays — Ibsen,
O'Neill — nothing under four hours. And Shakespeare —
didn't you love it?

ANDREW.   Sometimes. But I left.

DEIRDRE.   Why?

ANDREW.   *(Thrilled by the memory.)* *LA Medical!* The bucks! *TV
Guide.* My face at every supermarket check-out in America,
right next to the gum. I felt like — every day was my Bar
Mitzvah. Everyone I saw was smiling, with an envelope with a
check. That's what California is, it's one big hug — it's Aunt
Sophie without the pinch.

DEIRDRE.   Andrew, Jim Corman was terrific, but now you're
back.

ANDREW.   On a whim. The show was dead, I thought, okay,
try New York, why not? Take some classes, maybe do a new
play, ease back in. But now — this place. *(He gestures to the
apartment.)* *Hamlet.* That's not the plan.

DEIRDRE.   Of course it is! It's your old plan, your real one!
You know the only thing that would be better? Better than
Hamlet?

ANDREW.   The Cliff notes?

DEIRDRE.   *Romeo and Juliet.* Remember, when we did that
scene in class? *(Deirdre runs up the stairs to the roof, stopping at
the landing, which she will use as Juliet's balcony. Her acting should
be long on eagerness, if somewhat lacking in technique. She is very
big on expressive hand gestures. As Juliet.)*

    O, swear not by the moon,
       (She points to the moon.)
    the inconstant moon

(She points to the moon again.)
That monthly changes in her circled orb
Lest that thy love
(She points to Andrew.)
prove likewise variable.
(Andrew leaps up to the landing, with the bannister still separating him from Deirdre.)
ANDREW.   *(As Romeo.)* What shall I swear by?
DEIRDRE.   Do not swear at all,
Or if thou wilt, swear by thy gracious self
Which is the god of my idolatry,
And I'll believe thee.
ANDREW.   My heart's dear love ... *(Andrew climbs over the railing, and they kiss. Passionately.)* Oh, Deirdre ...
DEIRDRE.   Andrew ... *(Another kiss.)*
ANDREW.   Will you ... stay?
DEIRDRE.   Yes. Upstairs. Isn't there an extra room? On the roof?
ANDREW.   Deirdre.
DEIRDRE.   Andrew — you said you understood. I can only give myself to the man I'll love forever. The man I'll marry.
ANDREW.   So marry me!
DEIRDRE.   Andrew, that's so sweet.
ANDREW.   Why won't you take me seriously? I'm not just talking about sex. You believe in things. And you almost make me believe. You *are* Juliet.
DEIRDRE.   Exactly! And you'll be Hamlet! I can see it! *(Descending the stairs.)* Andrew, I do want to get married, and I do want to have sex, it's just ... I've waited so long. I have so much invested in this. I mean, if it wasn't absolutely perfect, it would all just be wasted. I'd feel so silly.
ANDREW.   *(Following her down the stairs.)* Deirdre, you're a 29-year-old virgin. And you tell everyone. I think fear of silliness is not the issue.
DEIRDRE.   Oh, but won't it be wonderful, once I know for sure? Won't you be glad that we waited?
ANDREW.   *(Kneeling beside her.)* Deirdre, sex *is* wonderful. Take my word. It's right up there with unicorns and pot-

pourri, And antique lace and bayberry-scented candles. Deirdre, even Laura Ashley had sex.

DEIRDRE.   That's true ...

ANDREW.   When will you know? When will you be sure?

DEIRDRE.   Soon ... maybe. I know I'm being impossible, but it's not that I'm a prude. I just want — everything! And it's happening!

ANDREW.   It is?

DEIRDRE.   Of course! You're going to be Hamlet, and I'm going to be ... *Ophelia.* Oh Andrew, could I audition? Would they let me?

ANDREW.   I guess I could ask them ...

DEIRDRE.   Would you? And it wouldn't be sleazy, because I'm not sleeping with you! Isn't that perfect?

ANDREW.   Deirdre, that's nuts. It's like ... show business for Mormons. *(Deirdre grabs her shoulderbag and runs up the stairs to the roof.)*

DEIRDRE.   It's going to be the best! Good night, sweet ...

ANDREW.   Don't say it! If I can't have sex, I don't know why I should play Hamlet.

DEIRDRE.   Sweet prince! *(Deirdre exits out the door to the roof.)*

ANDREW.   *(To the heavens.)* What is this — a test? No sex? Shakespeare? It's like high school! *(He goes to the phone and dials; he holds Lillian's bottle of champagne in his free hand. Into the phone.)* Lillian? It's Andrew. When you get back, please call the people at the theater. Tell them I'm cancelling. And I'll be back at the hotel tomorrow. So goodbye, Hamlet, and goodnight, Barrymore! *(Andrew opens the bottle of champagne. As the cork pops, thunder and lightning explode. The lights all go out, and the wind moans. The clock from the belltower tolls again. As much melodrama as possible. A spotlight hits the door to the roof, at the top of the stairs. The door swings open, and smoke pours out. A triumphant trumpet flourish is heard, followed by a grand musical processional, which should continue under Barrymore's entrance. A figure is silhouetted in the doorway to the roof. The spotlight illuminates the figure: it is John Barrymore, striking a dramatic, melancholy pose. He is dressed as Hamlet; he wears black tights, a black velvet tunic with a wide, slashed neck, and a jewelled belt from which a golden dagger hangs. A full-length cape swirls about him. He is phenomenally sexual and dashing; he is the very image of a sly, romantic hero. Barrymore lifts his head, still appearing quite severe. He smiles rakishly. He surveys the apartment; he's been gone a long time. He slowly descends the staircase, studying what has become of his former residence. Finally, Barrymore sees Andrew. Andrew is frozen, holding the champagne bottle. Barrymore smiles at him.*

BARRYMORE.   Dear fellow. *(Barrymore spots the bottle. He grabs a glass and heads for Andrew; he hasn't had champagne in ages. He holds out the glass, gesturing to the bottle.)* May I? *(Andrew remains frozen. He tries to speak; only choking sounds emerge from his throat.)* Pardon? *(Andrew tries to speak again, but cannot. He holds out the bottle; Barrymore takes it, fills his glass and drinks, with vast enjoyment.)*

ANDREW.   You're ... him.

BARRYMORE.   Am I?

ANDREW.   You're ... dead.

BARRYMORE.   You know, occasionally I'm not truly certain. Am I dead? Or just incredibly drunk?

ANDREW.   You're ... Barrymore.

BARRYMORE.   Yes. Although my father's given name was Blythe; he changed it when he became an actor, to avoid embarrassing his family. Your name?

ANDREW.   *(Still completely unnerved.)* Andrew. Rally. It's really Rallenberg. I changed it, to avoid embarrassing ... the Jews.

BARRYMORE.   *(Surveying the premises.)* Behold. My nest. My roost. *(Indicating where things had been, perhaps with musical cues.)* A grand piano. A renaissance globe. A throne.

ANDREW.   You're dead! You're dead! *What are you doing here?*

BARRYMORE.   Lad — I'm here to help.

ANDREW.   Wait — how do I know you're a ghost? Maybe you're just ... an intruder.

BARRYMORE.   *(Toying with him.)* Perhaps. Cleverly disguised as Hamlet. *(Andrew slowly sneaks up on Barrymore. He touches Barrymore's forearm. Barrymore is very nonchalant.)* Boo.

ANDREW.   But — I can touch you. My hand doesn't go through.

BARRYMORE.   I'm a ghost, Andrew. Not a special effect.

ANDREW.   But ... ghosts are supposed to have powers! Special powers!

BARRYMORE.   I just rose from the dead, Andrew. And how was *your* morning? Now shall I truly frighten you?

ANDREW.   *(Not impressed.)* I'm not afraid of you.

BARRYMORE.   Shall I cause your flesh to quake?

ANDREW.   *(Very cocky.)* You couldn't possibly.

BARRYMORE.   Shall I scare you beyond all human imagination?

ANDREW.   Go ahead and try.

BARRYMORE.   In just six weeks time, you will play Hamlet. *(Andrew screams.)*

ANDREW.   *(Genuinely terrified.)* Oh my God, you really are him, aren't you?

BARRYMORE.   John Barrymore. Actor. Legend. Seducer. Corpse.

ANDREW.   So — it worked. The seance. Felicia, her mother — she brought you back, from over there.

BARRYMORE.   Not at all. You summoned me.

ANDREW.   I did?

BARRYMORE.   As a link in a proud theatrical tradition. Every soul embarking upon Hamlet is permitted to summon an earlier player. From Burbage to Kean to Irving — the call has been answered.

ANDREW.   Wait — you mean you're here to help me play Hamlet? Because you did it?

BARRYMORE.   Indeed.

ANDREW.   Okay. Fine. Then the problem's solved. Because I'm not going to play Hamlet. No way. So you can just ... go back. To ... wherever.

BARRYMORE.   I'm afraid that's not possible.

ANDREW.   Why not?

BARRYMORE.   I cannot return, I will not be accepted, until my task is accomplished. Until you have ...

ANDREW and BARRYMORE.   Played Hamlet.

BARRYMORE.   Precisely.

ANDREW.   *(Completely floored.)* Oh no. Oh my God. You mean, if I don't go through with it ...

BARRYMORE.   Then I'm here to stay. Within these walls. Trapped for all time, with a television actor.

ANDREW.   Well, excuse me — I happen to be a very good television actor! And I don't need any dead ham bone to teach me about anything! Even if I were going to play Hamlet, which I'm not, I could do just fine! All by myself! *(Barrymore glares at Andrew. He removes a small leatherbound copy of* Hamlet *from a pouch on his belt, and tosses it to Andrew.)*

BARRYMORE.   Very well then. Hamlet. "To be or not to be."

ANDREW.   That happens to be the speech I did at my auditions. And I got the part. *(Andrew tosses the copy of* Hamlet *back to Barrymore.)*

BARRYMORE.   Proceed. *(Barrymore reclines full length on the couch. Andrew, very full of himself, decides to show Barrymore a thing or two. He strides U., and turns his back. He hunches over.)* Yes?

ANDREW.   I'm doing my preparation.

BARRYMORE.   Your ... preparation.

ANDREW.   Yes. My acting teacher taught me this. Harold Gaffney.

BARRYMORE.   Harold Gaffney?

ANDREW.   The creator of the Gaffney technique. Act To Win. I can't just do the speech cold, I have to get into character. I have to become Hamlet. I'm doing a substitution.

BARRYMORE.   A substitution?

ANDREW.   I'm thinking about something that really happened to me, so I can remember the emotion, and recreate it.

BARRYMORE.   And what are you remembering?

ANDREW.   It's a secret. Otherwise it won't work. Be quiet, I'm going to act.

BARRYMORE.   Why do I feel we should spread newspapers about? I'm sorry, I shall be silent. Out of deep respect. Road closed — man acting. *(Andrew turns, and moves D., facing out. He makes a small snuffling noise. He loosens up his shoulders, like a prizefighter shadow-boxing. He makes a few faces; he is being ultra-naturalistic, very Method. He makes an ungodly howling noise, then slaps his own face. He repeats this. Barrymore watches all this, appalled.)* You know, Andrew, I am dead, and I shall be for all eternity. But I still don't have all day. *(Andrew begins again. After a few lunges, he begins to speak. His forehead is furrowed with intensity; his speech patterns are reminiscent of a Brooklyn tough guy, in the Brando/deNiro mode.)*

ANDREW.   To be ... nah. *(He paces. A thought occurs.)* Or ... not ... to ... be. That, *that* is the question. Whoa. Whether ... *(He holds up a hand.)* Whether 'tis nobler ... huh ... in the mind, right ...

BARRYMORE.   Wrong.

ANDREW.   What?

BARRYMORE.   No.

ANDREW.   What "No?"

BARRYMORE.   No.

ANDREW.   No, what? No you disagree with my interpretation, no my interpretation wasn't clear, no you think I'm totally horrible?

BARRYMORE.   Yes.

ANDREW.   I'm horrible?

BARRYMORE.   At the moment. What were you doing?

ANDREW.   I was internalizing the role. I was finding an emotional through-line.

BARRYMORE.   Why?

ANDREW.   Why? So the character will come alive! So I'll achieve some sort of truth! *(Barrymore rises, aghast.)*

BARRYMORE.   Truth! Your performance — the pauses, the moans, all that you clearly consider invaluable — it's utterly appalling. We must never confuse truth with asthma.

ANDREW.   What?

BARRYMORE.   I understand the impulse, God help me, I lived just long enough for the introduction of truth into the modern theater. As I recall, it accompanied synthetic fibers and the GE Kitchen Of Tomorrow.

ANDREW.   Oh — so you just want me to ham it up.

BARRYMORE.   I beg your pardon?

ANDREW.   Hamming. Mugging. Over the top. Too big. Too ...

BARRYMORE.   *(With a grand gesture.)* Barrymore?

ANDREW.   Well, you did have that reputation. As someone

... larger than life.

BARRYMORE.   What size would you prefer? Gesture, passion
— these are an actor's tools. Abandon them, and the result?
Mere reality. Employ them, with gusto, and an artist's finesse,
and the theater resounds! I do not overact. I simply possess
the emotional resources of ten men. I am not a ham; I'm a
crowd! Andrew, who is Hamlet?

ANDREW.   A prince?

BARRYMORE.   A star.

ANDREW.   What?

BARRYMORE.   A star. The role is a challenge, but far more
— an opportunity. To shine. To rule. To seduce. To wit —
what makes a star?

ANDREW.   Talent? *(They exchange a look.)* Sorry, I wasn't
thinking.

BARRYMORE.   A thrilling vocal range? Decades of training?
The proper vehicle? *(He shakes his head, no.)* Tights.

ANDREW.   Tights?

BARRYMORE.   Tights. Where are you looking? Right now?

ANDREW.   I am not!

BARRYMORE.   Of course you are! The potato, the cucum-
ber, the rolled sock — this is the history of Prince Hamlet.

ANDREW.   You mean — you padded yourself?

BARRYMORE.   Unnecessary. Even for the balcony. *(Pause, as
he gazes upward.)* The second balcony.

ANDREW.   So Hamlet should be ... horny?

BARRYMORE.   Hamlet is a young man, a college boy, at his
sexual peak. Hamlet is pure hormone. Ophelia enters, that
most beguiling of maidens. Chastity is discussed.

ANDREW.   Please, don't joke. Not about chastity.

BARRYMORE.   Why? What?

ANDREW.   I can't talk about it.

BARRYMORE.   Oh dear. Your beloved? A problem?

ANDREW.   A nightmare. Five months.

BARRYMORE.   What?

ANDREW.   Nothing.

BARRYMORE.   Truly?

ANDREW.   Necking at the Cloisters. Picnics on Amish quilts.

Sonnets.

BARRYMORE. Not ... sonnets.

ANDREW. Yes. And I've been faithful. Totally. It's unnatural. Do you know what happens when you don't have sex?

BARRYMORE. No.

ANDREW. Thanks.

BARRYMORE. But why?

ANDREW. Why her, or why me? Deirdre won't have sex because ... she's not sure. Because she's the victim of a relentlessly happy childhood, which she fully expects to continue.

BARRYMORE. And you?

ANDREW. Me? Why do I put up with all this? Why have I begged Deirdre to marry me, practically since the day we met? Because, in the strangest way, she's the most passionate woman I've ever met. Because when she sees a homeless person, she gives them a fabric-covered datebook. Deirdre's just ... she makes me think that love is as amazing as it's supposed to be. She's romantic, which means she's insane. I know I love her, because I want to strangle her. Does that make sense?

BARRYMORE. Of course. A virgin goddess.

ANDREW. Please — don't encourage her.

BARRYMORE. She is to be treasured, and honored. I have known few such women in my sensual history. Perhaps only five hundred. They are the most adorable saints. But ... there are ways.

ANDREW. *(Eagerly.)* What?

BARRYMORE. No. It would be unthinkable.

ANDREW. *What?*

BARRYMORE. I could never condone such Casanova-like tactics. Such Valentino mesmerism.

ANDREW. Such Barrymore deceit.

BARRYMORE. *(Mortally offended.)* Cad.

ANDREW. Yes?

BARRYMORE. Knave.

ANDREW. Please?

BARRYMORE. Hamlet!

ANDREW. No! Stop with that.

BARRYMORE. Hamlet, to cunningly expose his father's

murder, feigns madness. To perfect the pose, he must spurn his beloved, the fair Ophelia. She is undone.

ANDREW. But doesn't she kill herself? I don't want to hurt Deirdre.

BARRYMORE. You'll be merciful.

ANDREW. No, that would be dishonest.

BARRYMORE. You would prefer, perhaps, some form of therapy? Continued discussion? What is the present-day epithet — "communication?" That absolute assassin of romance? *(The door to the roof swings open. Deirdre enters, in a long, Victorian, white cotton nightgown, carrying a book. Deirdre will not be able to see Barrymore. Spotting Deirdre; aglow.)* Ahh!

DEIRDRE. Andrew?

ANDREW. *(Surprised.)* Deirdre.

BARRYMORE. *(Gazing at Deirdre, appreciatively.)* Darling.

DEIRDRE. Who were you talking to? *(Andrew turns to Barrymore.)*

BARRYMORE. No. She has no need to see me.

ANDREW. *(To Deirdre.)* No one. I was just ... running my lines. The soliloquies.

DEIRDRE. I've been reading your Barrymore book. He was incredible.

BARRYMORE. Nymph.

DEIRDRE. But his life — it was so tragic. Did you know, he was a major alcoholic. Toward the end, when he couldn't find liquor, he would drink cleaning fluid.

BARRYMORE. A black lie!

DEIRDRE. And perfume.

BARRYMORE. As a chaser.

DEIRDRE. I mean, he was magnificent, but he was married four times.

BARRYMORE. I was?

DEIRDRE. He would fall madly in love with these women, and then he'd become insanely jealous. And then he'd cheat on them. Andrew — I want you to promise me something. I know that Barrymore is your hero, and that we should all worship him, but please — promise me you'll never be anything like him. *(Andrew stands at C., midway between Deirdre and*

29

Barrymore. Deirdre takes Andrew's hand.) Do you promise? *(Barrymore takes Andrew's other hand.)*

BARRYMORE. *(Beseechingly.)* Swear it.

ANDREW. Deirdre — maybe Barrymore wasn't so bad.

BARRYMORE. Maybe?

ANDREW. I mean, he was very talented, and I'm sure he had a few ...

BARRYMORE. Sterling attributes?

ANDREW. Good days. *(Deirdre is now seated, paging through the Barrymore book.)*

DEIRDRE. Oh, no. He was ... well, do you know, the first time he had sex, he was only fourteen?

BARRYMORE. Which book is this?

DEIRDRE. With his own stepmother. Can you imagine?

BARRYMORE. I'm a Freudian bonus coupon.

DEIRDRE. And after that, there was no stopping him, he must have been with every woman in New York. He was a matinee idol, before he did *Hamlet.* He starred in these trashy plays, and women would swoon, right in the aisles. There are these pictures of him ... *(She holds open the book.)* from when he was young. He was so ... cool.

ANDREW. Deirdre?

DEIRDRE. Look at this picture — it's him rejecting Ophelia. See, he wore all black, sort of open at the neck. And tights. *(Barrymore is delighted.)*

ANDREW. *(To Barrymore.)* Shut up!

DEIRDRE. *(Thinking Andrew was speaking to her.)* What? What do you mean? Oh, I get it. You're treating me the way Hamlet treats Ophelia. Andrew, do you think Hamlet slept with Ophelia?

BARRYMORE. Only in the Chicago company.

ANDREW. *(To Barrymore.)* Shut up!

DEIRDRE. *(Almost swooning.)* Oh, Andrew. Hamlet's so mean to Ophelia. He says, "Get thee to a nunnery." A nunnery! Oh, if you said that to me ... I'd die.

ANDREW. *(To Barrymore.)* I'm not kidding.

DEIRDRE. Oh Andrew, say it. Like in the play.

ANDREW. What? Get thee to a nunnery?

DEIRDRE.   No — like Barrymore!

BARRYMORE.   *(With tremendous authority.)* Barrymore. Begin! *(Barrymore begins another lesson. He gazes at Deirdre, and lightly strokes her face. Ghostly music. He turns away. He motions for Andrew to do the same. Andrew gazes at Deirdre, and strokes her face. No music. Andrew's actions are perfunctory; he tries not to participate. He gestures — "See? It didn't work."*

DEIRDRE.   *(Very disappointed.)* Andrew ... *(Barrymore is outraged at Andrew's lack of cooperation.)*

BARRYMORE.   *(Howling.)* GET THEE ... *(Andrew is shocked by Barrymore's roar; he moves into action, also at fever pitch.)*

ANDREW.   TO A NUNNERY! *(Deirdre is shocked and thrilled at this new Andrew.)*

DEIRDRE.   Yes!

BARRYMORE.   *(Still very passionate.)* Why wouldst thou be a breeder of sinners? *(Andrew has grabbed the copy of* Hamlet*; he hurries after Barrymore. Together they stalk Deirdre, with great sensual intensity.)*

ANDREW.   I am myself indifferent honest, but yet I could accuse me of such things ...

BARRYMORE.   Pause. Consider. Destroy!

ANDREW.   *(With enormous authority.)* ... that it were better my mother had not *born me!*

DEIRDRE.   *No!*

ANDREW.   I am very proud ...

BARRYMORE.   Revengeful ...

ANDREW.   With more offenses at my beck than I have thoughts to put them in ...

DEIRDRE.   *(Backing around the couch.)* Andrew, this is making me very nervous ...

ANDREW.   Imagination to give them shape, or time to act them in! *(Andrew takes Deirdre in his arms; they embrace and kiss with wild abandon. Barrymore stands nearby, urging them on and enjoying the spectacle.)*

BARRYMORE.   What should such fellows as I do crawling between earth and heaven? We are arrant knaves all, believe none of us! *(Andrew literally sweeps Deirdre off her feet. He carries her to the couch.)*

ANDREW.   Go thy ways to a nunnery! *(Andrew tosses Deirdre onto the couch; she reaches out to him. He regards her with majestic disdain, thoroughly rejecting her.) Call my machine!*

DEIRDRE.   No! *(Deirdre moans, and continues reaching out to Andrew, imploringly. Andrew turns to Barrymore; they shake hands, both very full of themselves and their success. Andrew turns back to Deirdre. She pleads.)* My lord Hamlet!

ANDREW.   Fair maiden. *(Andrew lowers himself onto the couch, into Deirdre's arms. They kiss passionately; just as things are about to progress, the doorbell buzzes. Unbearably frustrated.)* NO! *(The doorbell buzzes repeatedly.)* GO AWAY! *(Deirdre leaps up and goes to the intercom.)*

DEIRDRE.   *(Into phone, composing herself.)* Hello?

BARRYMORE.   Poor boy! Within one couplet! Shakespeare — the most potent aphrodisiac.

ANDREW.   *(In frantic despair.)* I was almost there! I was going to have sex!

DEIRDRE.   *(Still on the intercom.)* It's Gary!

BARRYMORE.   Gary?

ANDREW.   A friend. A director. From LA. He did my show. Why is he here? Why?

BARRYMORE.   You are Hamlet. A study in frustration. Thwarted action. *(Deirdre has opened the front door, and is peering out into the hall. Gary Peter Lefkowitz appears. Gary is in his thirties; he personifies LA shaggy-chic. He wears extremely expensive casual clothing; an Armani suit or a $5,000 suede jacket with a baseball cap. Gary should be played as an extremely happy, overgrown child, an oddly appealing creature of pure appetite. Reality is of very little consequence to Gary; the deal is all.)*

GARY.   Dee Dee!

DEIRDRE.   Gary! *(Gary and Deirdre hug.)* What are you doing here? Why aren't you in LA?

GARY.   I'm here for my man. My man Andrew Rally. Andy boy! *(Gary opens his arms to Andrew.)* Talk-time, Andy man. Fusion has occurred. Yes! *(Gary goes into a brief physical spasm, a celebratory combination of war dance and gospel fervor.)*

DEIRDRE.   I'll let you guys talk. I'm going to finish my reading. *(Deirdre begins ascending the stairs to the roof. She turns to Andrew, longingly.)* My liege?

ANDREW.   *(Disgruntled.)* Yeah, to a nunnery. *(Deirdre trembles visibly, and utters a passionate moan.)*

DEIRDRE.   Oooh! *(She runs upstairs and out the door to the roof.)*

GARY.   Reading? She's reading?

ANDREW.   I don't understand it.

GARY.   Still no...? *(He makes an obscene hand gesture denoting sexual intercourse.)*

ANDREW.   No, Gary. Still no hand gestures.

GARY.   Whoa. Man, if I was with a lady for that long, and there was still no return, I don't know, I might start thinking trade-in. Turn-around. And who's this? *(Gary gestures to Barrymore. Andrew looks at Barrymore, shocked that Gary can see him.)*

BARRYMORE.   Of course he can see me. Because it won't make any difference. *(Introducing himself to Gary.)* John Barrymore.

GARY.   Barrymore. Right. Disney? VP?

BARRYMORE.   No. I'm an actor.

GARY.   An actor! Whoa! Not another one. Good luck, big guy. I mean it. See, that's what's great about you guys. You're both actors, you're like in direct competition, but you can still give the appearance of friendship. See, I'm fucked up, I can't be friends with anyone like me.

BARRYMORE.   We understand.

GARY.   I mean, the way I monitor, there's only bungalow space for so many hyphenates, right?

BARRYMORE.   Hyphenates?

GARY.   Writer-producer-director. Gary Peter Lefkowitz.

BARRYMORE.   Ah. I see. So, if you also designed the scenery, would you require an additional name?

GARY.   Cute. That's cute. *(Admiring Barrymore's outfit.)* Great look. What is that? Japanese? Washed silk?

BARRYMORE.   Hamlet. Shakespeare.

GARY.   Right. Nice. Retro.

BARRYMORE.   Sixteenth century.

GARY.   Whoa. God, other centuries. Like, people who

weren't me. Okay, tell me, total truth, am I like the most self-obsessed person you've ever met? My answer? Yes. Okay, enough about me. Figure of speech. Andy, Andy boy, Andy my love — we got it. Green light. The go-ahead. Network approval! A pilot and five episodes!

ANDREW.   A pilot and five episodes — of what?

GARY.   Of the show! Of *our* show!

ANDREW.   What are you talking about?

GARY.   Okay, I didn't tell you. Because I didn't want you to be disappointed, and blame me, if it didn't go. But it went! I used your name to tip it through the hoop. I told the network it was your all-time favorite project, that you were ready to roll. And after Jim Corman, you're network candy, they're crawling.

ANDREW.   Really?

GARY.   America cries out! Your commitment was just the push!

BARRYMORE.   But he's not committed. He's playing Hamlet.

ANDREW.   Well ...

GARY.   Wait a second — which network?

BARRYMORE.   In the park. This summer.

GARY.   What, it's like for some special? Hallmark Hall Of Fame?

BARRYMORE.   It's not for anything. It's ... theater.

GARY.   Wait, let me get this. It's Shakespeare, right, it's like algebra on stage. And it's in Central Park, which probably seats, what, 500 tops. And the only merchandising involves, say, Gielgud cassettes and Mostly Mozart tote-bags. And on top of this, it's free. So Andy, tell me, who the hell is representing you nowadays?

ANDREW.   Lillian is all for it.

GARY.   Lillian! Jesus, of course. Andy, I love her, but she's a war criminal. I'm not kidding. She's a ten hour documentary waiting to happen. Okay Andy, fine, do your little show in the park. Is it a deduction? I mean, it's not even dinner theater. What, they sell whole wheat brownies and little bags of nuts and raisins. It's snack theater. It's Shakespeare for squirrels. Wait, just answer me one question, one simple thing: why? Why are you doing this? Are you broke?

ANDREW.   No. I have savings.

GARY.   Is there a bet involved?

ANDREW.   No!

GARY.   Andy — are you in some sort of trouble?

ANDREW.   Yes Gary, that's it, you finally hit it. Joe Papp has my parents.

GARY.   *Hamlet.* Andy, I have to say this, 'cause we're buds, and I cherish that budship — but think reputation. Word on the street. When folks — let's call 'em Hollywood — when they hear that you're doing the greatest play in the English-speaking world, they're gonna know you're washed up!

ANDREW.   Gary ...

GARY.   I'm serious. You haven't had offers? Nothing? What about the commercials? That Trailburst crap?

ANDREW.   Gary, have you ever seen those ads? Have you seen what I have to work with?

BARRYMORE.   What?

GARY.   A puppet. A furry little chipmunk. It's cute.

ANDREW.   It's a *hand puppet. (To Barrymore.)* Have you ever worked with a puppet? There's some guy, kneeling down near your crotch, working the puppet. And he's doing a chipmunk voice, into a microphone. And the guy, the chipmunk operator, he says, *(In a high-pitched, cutesy chipmunk voice.)* "Oh Andy, can I have a Trailburst Nugget?" And I say no, they're for people, not chipmunks. And he starts ... to cry. And I ... *(Andrew can't quite continue.)*

BARRYMORE.   You what?

ANDREW.   *(Mortified.)* I ... kiss him. On the top of his little chipmunk head.

GARY.   It's great!

ANDREW.   It's disgusting! It's humiliating! I didn't spend four years in college and two in drama school to end up comforting someone's fist! It's not even a decent product. Trailburst Nuggets are like sawdust dipped in chocolate, and they have more calories than lard.

GARY.   And that's why you're doing *Hamlet?*

ANDREW. Gary, you don't understand, about the theater. About why people do Shakespeare.

BARRYMORE. They do it because — it's art.

GARY. *(After a beat.)* Andy. Andy my honey, Andy my multi-talented prime-time delight. You don't do art. You buy it. You do TV, or a flick, you make a bundle and you nail a Monet. I was at this producer's place in Brentwood on the weekend. Incredible. Picassos. Van Gogh. A Rembrandt. And all from his TV shows.

ANDREW. But Gary, I don't want to just buy art. I mean, which would you rather do, paint a Picasso or own one?

GARY. Are you kidding? I'd like to sell one. At auction. Cash-flow. See, that's what I like — balls in the air. Activity. You're my Rembrandt.

ANDREW. I am?

GARY. How much are you gonna clear from this Shakespeare deal? Zip, right? Actually, you're paying them, because your time is valuable. A pilot and five episodes, high six figures. And if it hits, you get participation.

ANDREW. *(Impressed.)* Participation? In syndication?

GARY. Yup. You'll get paid every time it airs, first run, re-run, four AM in Singapore in the year 3000. Basically, you'll be able to afford to buy England, dig up Shakespeare, and get him to write the Christmas show!

BARRYMORE. This television program you're promoting, this goldmine — what is it exactly?

GARY. Okay — the pitch. Gather ye round. It's not cops, it's not young doctors, none of that TV crap.

ANDREW. Great.

GARY. You're a teacher. Mike Sullivan. You're young, idealistic, new to the system. Inner city high school. Rough. Dope. M-1's. Teen sex.

ANDREW. Wow ...

GARY. No one cares. All the other teachers are burn-outs. Not you.

BARRYMORE. Why not?

GARY. Because ... you care. You grew up in the neighborhood. You want to give something back.

ANDREW. *(Sincerely.)* You know, that sounds sort of ... okay. It's almost realistic. I mean, you could deal with real problems. I could be vulnerable. I could mess up sometimes.

GARY. And at night, after the sun goes down, you have superpowers.

BARRYMORE. Superpowers?

GARY. Sure. I mean, who wants to watch that caring-feeling-unwed mothers bullshit? It's over. But, after sundown, you're invincible. Modified x-ray vision. You can fly, but only about ten feet up. See, we're keeping it real. Gritty. And so, after dark, you help the community, you help the kids, with your powers.

ANDREW. Do they know it's me? When I have superpowers?

GARY. No. You're in leather, denim, they just think it's some great dude. Great title, killer title — *Night School.* Dolls. Posters. The clothes. You could get an album, easy.

ANDREW. But ... I can't sing.

GARY. Someone can. You can keep the Trailburst gig, there's no conflict — they'll probably extend, 'cause now you're a teacher! So think about it. What's to think, you've got a network commitment. Just forget this *Hamlet* crap — I mean, who are you kidding?

ANDREW. What do you mean?

GARY. Andy, I know you. I gave you your break. You're no actor.

ANDREW. What?

GARY. You're better than that. An actor, what, that's just some English guy who can't get a series. Look, I'm in town, I'm at the Ritz. I'll talk to Lillian, get things rolling. *(Gary hugs Andrew. He shakes Barrymore's hand.)* Great to meet you. You act, right?

BARRYMORE. John Sidney Barrymore.

GARY. We'll keep you in mind. Barrymore — any relation to the dead guy?

BARRYMORE. Distant.

GARY. *(At the door.)* Death. Man. Think about it — the third coast. *(Gary exits, out the front door.)*

ANDREW. *(Defensively.)* Don't say it! He's right, he's totally right!

BARRYMORE. *Night School?*

ANDREW. I don't know what to do! Think about the money — you had that kind of money!

BARRYMORE. Yes, as I grew older. Wealth is obscene in the young, it stunts ambition.

ANDREW. But ... but ... what about security?

BARRYMORE. What is this mania for security? What's the worst that can happen?

ANDREW. That I play Hamlet and Gary's right. And no one will hire me, and soon I'm face down in the gutter, wearing rags, without a job or anywhere to go.

BARRYMORE. Shouldn't every evening end like that?

ANDREW. Why am I talking to you? And it's not just the money, I'm not that superficial. It's the *fame.* Do you know how many people will watch *Night School,* even if it's a bomb?

BARRYMORE. Of course. There is fame in that sort of work. You may be admired, lusted after. You may acquire all the attributes of a well-marketed detergent. But there is fame — mere celebrity — and there is glory. Do you appreciate the difference?

ANDREW. Of course. Fame pays better. Fame has beach-front property. Fame needs bodyguards.

BARRYMORE. Glory, only an audience.

ANDREW. Oh, come on! That audience has changed! Don't you think that if Shakespeare were around now, he'd be writing normally?

BARRYMORE. I beg your pardon? *(Andrew grabs the* Hamlet *script.)*

ANDREW. You know, wouldn't the characters say, how are you, instead of how dost thou, my liege? What is a liege, anyway? And what's a fardel? In "To be or not to be," there's this line; Hamlet is thinking about suicide, right? And he tells about how awful life is, the whips and scorns of time.

BARRYMORE. Correct.

ANDREW. And he says, why should anyone put up with all this "when he himself might his quietus make with a bare bodkin." Quietus? Bodkin?

BARRYMORE. Quietus means death; a bodkin is a dagger.

ANDREW. And this next sentence, "Who would fardels bear..."

BARRYMORE. A fardel is a burden. Any burden.

ANDREW. So why can't we change it? Why can't I just say, so with all this garbage in the world, why not just stab yourself? Instead of dragging your fardels around? Then it would be clear, then people would get it!

BARRYMORE. Angels and ministers of grace, defend us! Tell me — if you loathe Shakespeare, if Los Angeles is so alluring — why did you audition?

ANDREW. Because my agent made me! And because Deirdre loves *Hamlet!* And because — because they asked me!

BARRYMORE. Because they asked you?

ANDREW. Because somewhere, someone thought that maybe, just maybe — I could do it. That I wouldn't have to be just Jim Corman, rookie surgeon, for the rest of my life. On TV, no one cared if I was talented, I had the right twinkle, the demographic appeal. And after a while, I started to think maybe that's all I had. That if I didn't show up, they could just use the poster. But I came to New York and somebody said, wait. Maybe Andy Rally could do Shakespeare. Onstage. Say those lines.

BARRYMORE. Act!

ANDREW. Yes. But they were wrong! I belong on TV, I know that. And it's not a crime. And I'm sorry I got you down here, and I'm sure that if you go back and talk to whomever, you can get this whole *Hamlet* deal cancelled. Because I'm really tired, and my girlfriend won't sleep with me, and I think my agent is very ill but she refuses to discuss it. And my life is an embarrassing joke, so if you'd please just leave, I'd appreciate it!

BARRYMORE. Can you imagine you're the first performer to experience such misgivings? Can you possibly believe that every prospective Hamlet did not tremble, and pale, and bolt? *Hamlet* will change you, Andrew, make no mistake. And the deal, as you term it, cannot be cancelled. And I cannot depart these premises until you have fulfilled your destiny. You approach a crossroads, and a decision must be made. What are you to be — artist, or lunchbox?

ANDREW.   Stop it!

BARRYMORE.   You are no longer Jim Corman.

ANDREW.   Get out.

BARRYMORE.   And you are not yet sensitive Mike Sullivan.

ANDREW.   You don't know that.

BARRYMORE.   You are Hamlet!

ANDREW.   No! *(Andrew and Barrymore are facing off; neither will give an inch. Barrymore finally makes a decision.)*

BARRYMORE.   Right! *(Barrymore strides to a tall, bulky object standing in a corner; the object is completely shrouded in a sheet. With a flourish, Barrymore tugs the sheet away, revealing a carved mahogany cabinet.)*

ANDREW.   *(Astonished.)* That's not mine! How did that get there? *(Barrymore opens the cabinet, and removes a sword, a duelling rapier. He tosses the sword to Andrew, who catches it.)* A sword? Oh my God. *(Barrymore strides to the opposite side of the room. He tugs a sheet from another shrouded object, revealing a suit of armor.)* I should call the movers. *(Barrymore removes a second sword from the suit of armor. He tests the sword, bending it, and then raises it above his head. He points it at Andrew.)*

BARRYMORE.   En garde!

ANDREW.   *What?*

BARRYMORE.   The drama's conclusion. Hamlet's duel and death. *(Barrymore begins to advance to Andrew, brandishing his sword.)*

ANDREW.   Excuse me? I can't fence.

BARRYMORE.   Hamlet can. I can. *(Barrymore takes a swipe at Andrew, who jumps back.)*

ANDREW.   Stop that! I hate swords! I hate violence! *(Barrymore takes another swipe. Andrew breaks away, rapidly.)* I have a gym excuse!

BARRYMORE.   As does Hamlet, until the closing moments of the drama. At last, he takes action. He assumes a tragic stature. *(Barrymore feints at Andrew, who jumps again.)*

ANDREW.   He dies!

BARRYMORE.   A hero! *(He slashes the air with his sword, bounding about in his best swashbuckling manner.)* This is why one acts! This is why actors are envied! We are allowed to *do* this sort of thing!

ANDREW.   Not anymore. We have stunt people. Doubles.

BARRYMORE.   Of course — for the soliloquies! *(Barrymore advances on Andrew, who runs and hides in the passage beneath the staircase. Andrew then backs out, on the other side of the staircase. Barrymore has anticipated this, and has circled around to meet him. The exact fight choreography is, of course, left to the discretion of any individual production. Barrymore feints at Andrew who, for the first time, raises his sword to defend himself.)* Well done!

ANDREW.   No! Stop it! I can't do this. *(Andrew lays down his sword. During Andrew's next speech, Barrymore might stand on the couch, bouncing and slashing the air with his sword, in a playful if dangerous mood.)* I'm stopping, okay? You're very cute, but I'm not going to play. You think you can force me to be like you, to be Hamlet. To be bold, and dashing, and vengeful. Well, no. I don't do that. I'm a liberal. So no duels. No macho behavior. Not in my house.

BARRYMORE.   *(Outraged.)* Your house! *(Barrymore leaps from the couch. He and Andrew face off. Barrymore raises his sword. Decisively, he slashes the couch, ruining the upholstery.)*

ANDREW.   *(In disbelief.)* My couch. You slashed my couch.

BARRYMORE.   It offended me. So modern. *(Barrymore looks around. He raises his sword, and sweeps a lamp off a table. It crashes to the floor.)*

ANDREW.   Stop it! That's my lamp! You're making a mess!

BARRYMORE.   Buy a new lamp! Residuals! *(Barrymore sweeps a vase off a shelf with his sword; the vase shatters. Alternately, and to save money, Barrymore might pick up a vase and hurl it offstage, through the archway, from which appropriate crashing noises might issue. Andrew, livid at the destruction of his property, picks up his sword and brandishes it. He becomes a decisive man of action.)*

ANDREW.   That's enough! The girl doesn't come until Friday! *Someone is going to vacuum!*

BARRYMORE. *(Delighted.)* Not I! *(Barrymore gestures, and excit-ing, galloping swordfight music begins, very Errol Flynn. He and Andrew begin some serious fencing. Andrew lunges at Barrymore; they cross swords, above their heads.)*

ANDREW. Again! *(Andrew and Barrymore fence, moving across the stage. Barrymore fences with one hand, and swigs from the bottle of champagne with the other. At one point, Barrymore uses the bottle to fence with.)*

BARRYMORE. Nicely done! *(Barrymore shakes the bottle of cham-pagne, and sprays Andrew with the fizz. They continue to fence, with great brio, all over the stage. Andrew backs Barrymore up the stair-case. He disarms Barrymore, whose sword falls. Andrew's sword is now at Barrymore's throat.)*

ANDREW. Say it! Say I don't have to do it! No Hamlet!

BARRYMORE. But Andrew — you're already doing it. Look! *(Andrew is distracted, and Barrymore kicks the sword out of Andrew's hand, grabbing it for himself. He backs Andrew down the stairs, at swordpoint. Gleefully.)* Hamlet — rookie prince! *(Andrew retrieves Barrymore's previous sword, and they continue to fence.)* Hamlet?

ANDREW. I can't!

BARRYMORE. Then shall I kill you? *(Barrymore knocks the sword from Andrew's hand; Andrew is now defenseless, as Barrymore advances on him.)* Right now? Curtail your precious mediocrity? Imagine your epitaph — "Andrew Rally, Beloved Coward. Be-loved Hack. Here Lies No One!" *(Barrymore feints at Andrew, and seemingly wounds him. Andrew clutches himself and moans; he slumps to the floor. His injury is highly believable. Barrymore is aghast; he had not intended to actually hurt Andrew.)* Lad?

ANDREW. *(Trying to speak, clearly in great pain.)* No ... you're right ...

BARRYMORE. *(Kneeling.)* What? Are you ... shall I call some-one? A physician?

ANDREW. No.

BARRYMORE. I'm sorry, I didn't intend to ... wound you.

ANDREW. *(Barely able to speak.)* Call ...

BARRYMORE. Call whom? Deirdre? *(Andrew leaps to his feet, fully recovered and triumphant. He grabs his sword and points it at*

42

Barrymore.)
ANDREW.   Shakespeare!
BARRYMORE.   Ha! *(Barrymore grins, and makes an arm gesture; a jubilant trumpet flourish is heard.)*

CURTAIN

ACT TWO

Scene 1

Place: The same.

Time: Opening night, six weeks later.

The apartment has been transformed, into a true medieval lair. All of Andrew's furniture has been replaced by elaborately carved, heavy dark oak pieces. There is a richly upholstered chaise, and an ottoman center stage. An ornate throne sits off to one side, and the glorious fireplace is now fully revealed. A tapestry hangs on one wall, with a chandelier above. A renaissance globe stands near the staircase. The floor is covered with oriental carpets, stacks of antique leatherbound books, and atmospheric mounds of brocade cushions. Various candelabra and sconces are located around the room, as yet unlit. The suit of armor and other appropriately Gothic pieces complete the lavishly theatrical mood.

Several vases of flowers have been placed about; other boxes of flowers are stacked by the front door.

As the curtain rises, Barrymore descends from the roof, singing to himself. He crosses to the globe, which opens to reveal a fully-stocked bar. Barrymore pours himself a drink. He is still dressed as Hamlet.

Felicia enters, very dressed up, from the archway. She cannot see Barrymore. She stares at the apartment's new furnishings, shaking her head.

FELICIA.   Oh my God. What got into him? *(Deirdre enters, also from the archway, carrying a vase of flowers. Deirdre is dressed in a flowing velvet, medieval-style gown, complete with a lengthy train and trailing sleeves. She is playing one of Ophelia's ladies-in-waiting, and a wreath of flowers has been braided into her hair.)*

DEIRDRE.   Isn't it incredible? It's Barrymore! Andrew says this is exactly what it used to look like! He says it's been helping him, to get in the mood.

FELICIA.   Well I hope he's there — in the mood. It's opening night! *(Deirdre and Felicia shriek with excitement. They are wildly excited; this entire scene should be played with an air of giddy anticipation and suspense.)*

DEIRDRE.   Opening night! *Hamlet!*

FELICIA.   So where is he? Doesn't he have to get to the theater?

DEIRDRE.   He's upstairs, getting ready, on the roof. He's in costume, too, he wears it everywhere. And he talks to Barrymore.

FELICIA.   Really? He got through?

DEIRDRE.   No, he just imagines. I catch him at it all the time. Do you think he's here? Watching over us?

FELICIA.   Barrymore?

DEIRDRE.   Yes! Oh John Barrymore, wherever you are! Bless this evening! Bless Andrew! *(As Deirdre invokes Barrymore, she runs through the room, seeking the ghost. Barrymore follows her, skipping along behind her, highly amused. Finally he stretches out on the chaise.)*

FELICIA.   Honey, you better calm down. *(Barrymore beckons to Deirdre from the chaise. He opens his arms.)*

DEIRDRE.   I know, I've been like this all day, all week, I can't sit still ... *(Deirdre, pulled by unseen forces, sits on the chaise beside Barrymore. She lies down, as he gently strokes her hair. She is unaware of his presence, but he has his effect.)* Felicia, what's it like? Sex? *(Felicia is busily putting finishing touches on her makeup, inspecting herself in the mirror of her compact.)*

FELICIA.   Sex? Oh, that's right — you're still on the bench. No wonder you're nervous. Sex is great. With the right guy.

DEIRDRE.   Really? But what about with the wrong guy?

FELICIA.   *(After a beat.)* Better.

DEIRDRE.   Felicia, you're terrible! *(Barrymore kisses Deirdre's neck.)* Stop it!

FELICIA. What? *(Deirdre leaps up, flustered. Barrymore rises as well, and heads for the staircase.)*

DEIRDRE. *(Unnerved.)* Nothing. Felicia — how do you know? If you're really in ultimate love? If it's ... Shakespeare?

FELICIA. What's to know? Andy's the best. I mean, he's a star, he must have girls coming outta the woodwork. And he's waiting for you.

DEIRDRE. That's true. It's just — sometimes I think I'll never marry anyone. I mean, anyone alive. *(Barrymore, on the staircase, turns and salutes Deirdre's last phrase — "anyone alive." He raises his glass in a toast. Then he heads up the stairs and exits to the roof.)*

FELICIA. Hon?

DEIRDRE. I've always wanted to be Joan of Arc, or Juliet, or Guinevere. And I want to love someone like Hamlet, or King Arthur, or Socrates.

FELICIA. You're rich, right?

DEIRDRE. No — why?

FELICIA. Well, the way you think, I mean I love it, but, you don't have to make a living, right?

DEIRDRE. No, I'm not rich, really. Just my parents. They're so great, they've been married for almost forty years. And that's what I want — eternal love! For the ages! And tonight, Andrew's playing Hamlet. And I'll know. *(Gary enters, from the archway, carrying a glass and a bottle of champagne. He wears a tuxedo, a model both luxurious and trendy.)* Gary, that's bad luck! The champagne is for afterwards, to celebrate!

GARY. Oh, sorry. *(Deirdre grabs the champagne from Gary and exits through the archway, leaving Gary alone with Felicia.)* Hey — big night! Hot stuff!

FELICIA. I can't wait!

GARY. You know, I love Andy, he's a great actor, but — what if he really sucks? *(Deirdre re-enters.)*

DEIRDRE. He won't! He's going to be glorious! Don't even think that!

FELICIA. I hope he's good. Although, you know, with Shakespeare — how can you tell?

GARY. Exactly. I mean, maybe it's foolproof — maybe, with Shakespeare, there's no difference between bad and good. And everybody's afraid to say it. I mean, at the movies, on the tube — either you're funny, or you're cancelled. You're good-looking, or you're best-supporting. I mean, you can tell. But Shakespeare — it's just real hard to tell who's good, without nudity.

DEIRDRE. Gary — have you ever been to the theater?

GARY. Yeah. Not lately. Can I be frank? I don't get it. The theater. It doesn't make sense. It's like, progress, right? Take it step by step. Back in Neanderthal times, entertainment was like, two rocks. Boom boom. Then, in the Middle Ages, they had theater. Then came radio. Then silent movies. Then sound. Then TV. That's like, art perfected. When you watch TV, you can eat. You can talk. You don't really have to pay attention, not if you've seen TV before. Nice half-hour chunks. Or even better, commercials. Thirty seconds. Hot girl, hot guy, the beer, it's all there. It's distilled. I mean, when I go to the theater, I sit there, and most of the time I'm thinking — which one is my armrest? *(The door to the roof swings open. Andrew appears, dressed as Hamlet, in a black costume similar to, although not identical, to Barrymore's. Andrew's Hamlet might have modern touches, but it must include tights and a codpiece, as well as a sword and a dagger. Andrew has been drinking, although he is by no means drunk. His vocal and physical style now resemble Barrymore's; he has acquired a grandeur, and is somewhat larger than life. He carriers a bottle of champagne.)*

ANDREW. OUT!

DEIRDRE. Andrew!

GARY. Big guy!

ANDREW. Out! Tonight I shall play Hamlet. I must be alone.

DEIRDRE. Andrew, honey, can't we take you to the theater?

ANDREW. Nay! I have dressed, I have drunk, I seek only solitude. *(Andrew stands on the landing halfway up the stairs. Gary climbs the stairs to meet him.)*

GARY. I hear you. And Andy, it's working like a charm. I told the network, Andy's not sure. He's thinking, he's doing

Hamlet — they love it. They know it's a trick. So I'm going for half-ownership of the show — or you'll do Lear.

ANDREW.   AWAY!

GARY.   *(Imitating Andrew, delighted.)* AWAY! I love this guy! Hey, what does opening night mean? A party?

DEIRDRE.   Of course.

GARY.   Photographers?

FELICIA.   Really?

GARY.   Critics?

DEIRDRE.   Andrew, don't listen! They'll love you, and it's not important!

GARY.   Not in movies or TV. That's the great thing — you can really blow, and no one can stop you. But tonight — watch out, right? They're out there! *(Gary starts moving back down the stairs. As he turns his back on Andrew, Andrew pulls out his dagger and points it at Gary's back; Gary does not see this, and Andrew returns his dagger to its sheath. Reaching C.)* You know, when I heard you were goin' through with this, I went, hey, maybe Andy's right. Maybe I should just chuck everything, leave LA, just produce, direct and write Shakespeare. But I woke up. Your turn, Andy boy. I gotta car downstairs — anybody?

FELICIA.   A car? A limo?

GARY.   You do real estate, right? You gotta come to Beverly Hills.

FELICIA.   I know, I dream about it. Beverly Hills — that's my *Hamlet.*

ANDREW.   NOW!

GARY.   We're going, we're going!

FELICIA.   We'll see you after. *(She takes a last look at Andrew; she is enraptured.)* Look at you! You are so adorable! Just like Peter Pan, but for evening!

ANDREW.   Farewell! *(Gary and Felicia exit, out the front door.)*

DEIRDRE.   Are you sure you don't want me to stay? I'll go with you, to the theater.

ANDREW.   Be gone, wench. *(Andrew comes down the stairs. As he does so, Deirdre gets her first good look at his codpiece. She blushes, and looks away, then steals a second glance. Andrew unsheathes his sword, and practices a few feints. Deirdre picks up a pair of oversized, extremely modern high-topped sneakers, Reeboks, which she has hidden behind the staircase. She carries the sneakers to the throne, and sits. During her next speech, she will remove her period slippers, and put on the enormous sneakers.)*

DEIRDRE.   I know you're going to be — the best. And I'm so proud of you. And I'm so glad we're in the play together, even if I am just one of Ophelia's ladies-in-waiting. And even if I don't have any lines. The director took me aside yesterday, at the dress rehearsal. He said I was very good, but that when they announce that Ophelia is dead, I shouldn't scream. Or stagger. Or grab your sword and try to stab myself. He said the play wasn't called "The Tragedy Of Ophelia's Best Friend." But I understand. *(Deirdre now has her sneakers on. Daintily holding her skirt, she walks toward the front door, past Andrew.)*

ANDREW.   My lady.

DEIRDRE.   My Lord. *(Andrew takes Deirdre's hand, and twirls her into a passionate embrace, with Deirdre bent backward. He then twirls her out of the embrace, and her sleeves whirl around her. Deirdre steadies herself, almost swooning. She glances at Andrew, and moans voluptuously. Deirdre goes to the front door. With her back to Andrew, she gathers her long, unwieldy skirts into a huge ball in her lap. She turns, carrying her bundle. She gives Andrew one last torrid look, and exits. Barrymore appears at the door to the roof. He carries a bottle of champagne, and salutes Andrew. They are now grand, lusty, Elizabethan comrades, bold and dashing.)*

ANDREW.   Blythe!

BARRYMORE.   Rallenberg!

ANDREW.   Tonight — *Hamlet!*

BARRYMORE.   The Dane!

ANDREW.   The Bard!

BARRYMORE.   The bottle!

ANDREW.   The best! *(Barrymore has now descended the stairs, and the men toast each other ceremoniously.)*

BARRYMORE.   And Deirdre!

ANDREW.   Deirdre?

BARRYMORE.   For certain. She shall witness your portrayal. She imagines herself Ophelia. She shall wed you, or drown.

ANDREW. We have accomplished much!

BARRYMORE. Vocal assurance.

ANDREW. *(Gesturing with his sword.)* Physical technique.

BARRYMORE. Even, dare I say it, an appreciation of the text.

ANDREW. Indeed. Our achievement is twofold — not only do I revere the play, but for the first time, I have finished it.

BARRYMORE. Welcome Rallenberg — to the royal order of Hamlets. *(The two men stride forward, their arms around each other's shoulders.)*

ANDREW. The elite!

BARRYMORE. The august!

ANDREW. Princes and players.

BARRYMORE. We do not step ...

ANDREW. We *stride.*

BARRYMORE. We do not speak ...

ANDREW. We beseech ...

BARRYMORE. We whisper ...

ANDREW. We roar!

BARRYMORE. Brother Hamlet!

ANDREW. *(With a deep bow.)* Player King.

BARRYMORE. The moment is nigh. I name my rightful heir. Kneel, Rally! *(During Andrew's investiture, and perhaps during the preceding scene, glorious, Pomp-And-Circumstance style music might be used as underscoring, emphasizing the evening's ritual aspects. Andrew kneels before Barrymore. Barrymore uses his champagne bottle as a sword, tapping Andrew on each shoulder.)* I hereby dub thee Prince Hamlet, of all lower Manhattan. You join an illustrious line. You shall henceforth be known as the greatest American Hamlet.

ANDREW. Of all time?

BARRYMORE. Of your generation. *(Andrew stands, a bit unsteadily. The reality of his situation is beginning to catch up with him.)*

ANDREW. Of my generation?

BARRYMORE. And why not?

ANDREW. It's just, I keep thinking ... tonight.

BARRYMORE. Of course — the performance. Minutes from

now.

ANDREW. No, no, I'm fine, I'm fine. Hamlet. Whoa. Hamlet.

BARRYMORE. Glory!

ANDREW. Glory ...

BARRYMORE. Shakespeare!

ANDREW. Shakespeare ...

BARRYMORE. Blind, unspeakable terror!

ANDREW. That's it!

BARRYMORE. Of course you're shaking. And for the noblest of reasons. The role. The moment. The test.

ANDREW. Come with me. Be there.

BARRYMORE. I cannot. You know that.

ANDREW. Then help me. There must be some ... ancient secret of the Hamlets. A trick, something you've been saving.

BARRYMORE. Of course. *(Barrymore looks around, checking to see that no one is listening. He seats Andrew, perhaps on a pile of cushions on the floor. Barrymore sits beside him, on the throne, as if about to impart confidential information.)* Speak the speech, I pray you, as I pronounced it to you, trippingly on the tongue. But if you mouth it, as many of our players do, I had as lief the town crier spoke my lines. Nor do not saw the air too much with your hand, thus, but use all gently; for in the very torrent, tempest, and, as I may say, whirlwind of your passion, you must acquire and beget a temperance that may give it smoothness. Be not too tame neither, but let your own discretion be your tutor. Suit the action to the word, the word to the action, with this special observance, that you o'erstep not the modesty of nature. For anything so o'erdone is from the purpose of playing, whose end, both at the first and now, was and is to hold as 'twere the mirror up to nature, to show virtue her own feature, scorn her own image, and the very age and body of the time his form and pressure. Now this overdone or come tardy off, though it makes the unskillful laugh, cannot but make the judicious grieve. Go make you ready. *(Barrymore has delivered the speech magnificently. Andrew rises, quite shaken.)*

ANDREW. I don't think so.

BARRYMORE. Go make you ready. It's all there. In the text. At your service.

ANDREW. I can't do that. What you just did. I'm ... who do I think I am?

BARRYMORE. Andrew — your fear has a history. *My* opening night — good Lord.

ANDREW. But — you were Barrymore.

BARRYMORE. Barrymore? I was a light comedian, attempting Olympus. There was a family reputation knotted about my neck. Before the curtain rose I sat on the stage in darkness, paralyzed with fear.

ANDREW. But you weren't ... some TV clown. You were still doing theater.

BARRYMORE. Don't overestimate the form. Would you like the titles of my boulevard triumphs? *The Fortune Hunter. Claire de Lune. Princess Zim Zim.*

ANDREW. But — what if Gary's right? What if the critics hate me?

BARRYMORE. *(Scornfully.)* Oh, newspapers.

ANDREW. What if *I* hate me?

BARRYMORE. You have prepared for this evening.

ANDREW. But, when you played Hamlet, you prepared for six months. In the country. Just learning the role.

BARRYMORE. You have been diligent.

ANDREW. Sure, but — six weeks? And tonight — people are gonna be there. Not just critics — my friends. My family. People who saw me in my second grade school play. And who might expect an improvement. And Deirdre.

BARRYMORE. She'll adore you.

ANDREW. It's not automatic. Deirdre wants me to be ... a hero. An immortal. What if that doesn't happen, what if I disappoint her?

BARRYMORE. Impossible!

ANDREW. Up till now I've been plugging away, trying to be Hamlet, trying to be like you, but now ...

BARRYMORE. Andrew — this is not your first opening night. Your panic, your doubt — this is all to be expected.

ANDREW. This isn't just stage fright. This is ... something

else.

BARRYMORE.   What?

ANDREW.   Common sense! I had this idea, that I could come back to New York, that I could prove some ridiculous point, to myself, to everybody. Instant actor! Just add Shakespeare! But I don't think it works that way!

BARRYMORE.   And why not?

ANDREW.   Because I'm going to be on that stage with real actors, with people who know what they're doing! Jesus, why did I listen to you? I could be in LA right now! Making a fortune! In pants!

BARRYMORE.   Is that what you'd like? Is that what I've taught you?

ANDREW.   That's what I know!

BARRYMORE.   Enough! You unbearable brat! Your snivelling is a disgrace! The words of Shakespeare — be worthy! The role of Hamlet — be grateful!

ANDREW.   Oh, come off it!

BARRYMORE.   What?

ANDREW.   Listen to yourself!

BARRYMORE.   Excuse me?

ANDREW.   After you played Hamlet, you left the theater! And you never came back!

BARRYMORE.   Unimportant! *(Andrew begins to stalk Barrymore, as their fight grows increasingly brutal.)*

ANDREW.   I read about it — after 101 performances, you went right to Hollywood!

BARRYMORE.   For a time!

ANDREW.   For the rest of your life!

BARRYMORE.   That is my affair!

ANDREW.   You lived in a mansion, in Beverly Hills. With a yacht, and a screening room, and — how many wives?

BARRYMORE.   Quite a few!

ANDREW.   You made movie after movie ...

BARRYMORE.   Some of them classics!

ANDREW.   Most of them garbage!

BARRYMORE.   Yes! And after awhile I even had trouble with those! *(A beat.)* There was a day, on a set, when the cameras rolled, and ... I couldn't remember a line. Nothing. Take after take. Not a word, not a speech, just haze and then — terror. And I wasn't drunk, no, stone sober. And everyone was more than kind, and the words were scribbled on shirt-sleeves, and cardboards held just out of camera range. But I knew — I knew instantly — I could never go back on the stage.

ANDREW. *(Maliciously.)* John Barrymore, the great classical actor! The example to us all!

BARRYMORE. The hopeless, unemployable lush! The public embarrassment! The off-color joke! *(With vicious intensity.)* Yes, I ran to Hollywood, you're quite right — and you can't imagine the life I led! I was a movie star, do you know what that means? My face five stories high, and six zeroes wide! *(A pause.)* But before all that, in my prime — I faced the dragon. I accepted a role so insanely complex, so fantastic and impossible, that any attempt is only that — an attempt! And I stood in the light, before a crowd fully prepared to dismiss, to deride, and to depart. And I shook them, I wooed them, and I said, yes, you will stay, and yes, you will remember! And for one moment in my life, I used all that I knew, every shred of talent, every ounce of gall! I was John Barrymore! And for those sacred evenings, there was no shame. I played Hamlet! Have you? *(By the end of this speech Barrymore is utterly drained; he staggers to a chair. His battle with Andrew has stunned both of them, and neither can speak. After a pause, the doorbell buzzes. Andrew goes to the intercom.)*

ANDREW. *(Into the receiver.)* Yes? Okay, okay, I'm coming. *(A moment passes between Andrew and Barrymore. Then Andrew opens the front door. Lillian steps into the room. She looks quite beautiful, in a silvery evening gown. She is very angry.)*

LILLIAN. Rally! The car is waiting! Go! *(Andrew looks to Barrymore for some final word. None is forthcoming.)* Go! *(Andrew runs out the door. Lillian turns, and sees Barrymore. To Barrymore.)* You. You look terrible.

BARRYMORE. *(Surprised that Lillian can see him.)* What? *(Andrew sticks his head back in.)*

ANDREW. Lillian — are you coming?

LILLIAN. I will catch up — in a cab.

ANDREW. Lillian — I have to do this, don't I?

LILLIAN. No. You can stay here, and cancel the production. I'd be so proud. Go! *(Andrew leaves. Lillian faces Barrymore.)* Yes, I can see you, you swine.

BARRYMORE. How?

LILLIAN. I am very old. I see everything. And it so happens I know you.

BARRYMORE. You do?

LILLIAN. Ha! I knew you would not remember.

BARRYMORE. *(As he stares at her.)* Could it be?

LILLIAN. *(Challenging.)* What?

BARRYMORE. No. Yes. Is it ... you?

LILLIAN. I was very young.

BARRYMORE. A young wife. Of ... a conductor.

LILLIAN. A violinist.

BARRYMORE. A violinist. Yes. With a mistress.

LILLIAN. Bravo.

BARRYMORE. *(Circling her.)* I was in town promoting a film. There was a cocktail party. Your husband was to meet you. He did not.

LILLIAN. Do not be smug. You were married as well. To an actress.

BARRYMORE. To an actress? Is that legal? I found you sobbing, in a coatroom.

LILLIAN. I did not sob!

BARRYMORE. Out of anger. We came here.

LILLIAN. Out of madness. Temporary insanity.

BARRYMORE. We had a fire. *(Barrymore makes a sweeping gesture, and a fire springs up in the fireplace.)*

LILLIAN. And candlelight. *(Barrymore makes another gesture, and all the candles, located throughout the room, suddenly glow. The stage lights dim, creating an impossibly romantic mood. A moon might appear at the window.)*

BARRYMORE. We stole champagne, from the party.

LILLIAN. And bought chocolate bars, from the five and dime.

BARRYMORE. We broke every commandment. We made love.

LILLIAN.   And gained weight.

BARRYMORE.   *(Delighted.)* You were impossible.

LILLIAN.   You were ... Barrymore. *(The mood has become very intimate; Barrymore and Lillian are almost in an embrace. Barrymore breaks away.)* What?

BARRYMORE.   No!

LILLIAN.   What is the matter?

BARRYMORE.   You are far too kind. I am undeserving. I have failed utterly. I return for a single purpose, and now ...

LILLIAN.   What? What is your purpose?

BARRYMORE.   That Andrew should play Hamlet.

LILLIAN.   So? It is done.

BARRYMORE.   But there's more, so much more. I wanted Andrew ... to learn.

LILLIAN.   To learn what?

BARRYMORE.   From all that he accuses me of! From my sorry excuse for a life! I was offered — the planet. Every conceivable opportunity. Andrew is my last vain hope. My cosmic lunge at redemption.

LILLIAN.   Tell me, Barrymore — when did it happen?

BARRYMORE.   What?

LILLIAN.   When did you turn — scoutmaster?

BARRYMORE.   Excuse me?

LILLIAN.   Rally is a big boy. You have pushed him, as have I. He needed that. But — tonight must be his. And his alone.

BARRYMORE.   So why do you stay? What do you want?

LILLIAN.   I am like anyone else. I have come to see Barrymore.

BARRYMORE.   A sideshow.

LILLIAN.   A three-ring circus. A true oddity. A movie star, and a Danish prince. A womanizer, but never a beast. A drunkard, but — at least until recently — never a bore. Tonight I had hoped for — one last encounter. An encore. But it was long ago. Perhaps I remember incorrectly. I will go. *(She starts to leave.)*

BARRYMORE.   Lillian?

LILLIAN.   *(Pausing.)* Yes?

BARRYMORE.   Will he be all right? Andrew?

LILLIAN.   Who can say?

BARRYMORE.   Have I helped him? In any way?

LILLIAN.   Ask him. When he returns. Any more questions?

BARRYMORE.   Just one. Your husband — is he well?

LILLIAN.   I hope not. We are divorced. You were named in the lawsuit.

BARRYMORE.   *(Pleased.)* Divorced ... *(After a beat.)* One last encounter? *(Barrymore gestures. Music — a lush, sweepingly romantic melody begins. Barrymore holds out his arms. Lillian resists.)*

LILLIAN.   I am old.

BARRYMORE.   I am dead.

LILLIAN.   I no longer dance.

BARRYMORE.   Make an exception.

LILLIAN.   Fool.

BARRYMORE.   Fraulein.

LILLIAN.   My Hamlet. *(Lillian goes to Barrymore. They dance. They pause.)* Tell me — where one goes, where you have come from — I am assuming it is heaven?

BARRYMORE.   Sad to say.

LILLIAN.   Is there ... smoking?

BARRYMORE.   Of course. It's heaven.

LILLIAN.   Should I ... be afraid?

BARRYMORE.   Of death? Never. Only of life.

LILLIAN.   Actors.

BARRYMORE.   *(Offended.)* What?

LILLIAN.   I love them. *(They continue to dance. They pause.)*

BARRYMORE.   You know, Lillian, there is another question that many ask. A question regarding certain activities, and their practice in the next world.

LILLIAN.   You mean, activities of a physical nature.

BARRYMORE.   Aren't you curious?

LILLIAN.   Surprise me. *(Barrymore laughs. They begin to dance again, as the lights dim, and the curtain falls.)*

Scene 2

Place: The same.

Time: 7 AM, the next morning.

Barrymore is slumped on the chaise, his shirt open and askew. He is surrounded by junk food wrappers and open bags of chips. A small portable TV is balanced on the ottoman. The romantic song from Barrymore's dance with Lillian now comes from the TV.

The music is interrupted by the Trailburst Nuggets TV commercial. Barrymore watches the commercial, transfixed and appalled.

CHIPMUNK.   *(On TV.)* Please Andy — can I have a Trailburst Nugget?
ANDREW'S VOICE.   *(On TV.)* I'm sorry — Nuggets are for people, not chipmunks. *(The chipmunk cries, loudly.)* Oh, all right, but remember — Trailburst Nuggets are a delicious breakfast treat. And an anytime snack. *(The Trailburst Nuggets jingle plays. Andrew has entered the apartment, quietly. He sings along with himself on the commercial. Andrew is still dressed as Hamlet, but he also wears sunglasses, a denim Levi's jacket and sneakers. Once Barrymore realizes Andrew is in the room, he shuts off the TV and leaps to his feet.)*
BARRYMORE.   *(Eagerly.)* Yes?
ANDREW.   *(After a pause.)* Yeah?
BARRYMORE.   The morning after! So?
ANDREW.   So?
BARRYMORE.   Your performance! Tell me! *(Andrew exits through the archway, further frustrating Barrymore.)* What, am I to remain despised? An ogre beyond question? Denied the result of my labor, forbade so much as a word, some meager report? *(Andrew re-enters from the archway, swigging from a carton of orange*

58

juice. He has removed his sunglasses.)

ANDREW.   So ... you want to know? What happened? Last night?

BARRYMORE.   If you wish to impart the information. If you have not grown too grand, too swollen with triumph.

ANDREW.   Who writes you?

BARRYMORE.   Tell me! I've earned it!

ANDREW.   *(After a pause.)* First — you tell me. Your deal, up there. Once I've played Hamlet, you can go back, right?

BARRYMORE.   Correct.

ANDREW.   And we'll never have to see each other again, right?

BARRYMORE.   Agreed.

ANDREW.   So nothing depends on ... the quality of the performance.

BARRYMORE.   I don't believe so. Why?

ANDREW.   Because ... it did not go very well. In fact — I was awful.

BARRYMORE.   *(Refusing to believe him.)* No.

ANDREW.   Sorry. I mean, I got through it, I remembered my lines. But — that's about all.

BARRYMORE.   Impossible. This is all modesty. I'm sure you were marvelous.

ANDREW.   I wasn't. Take my word. Or ask around. It wasn't a fiasco, but maybe that would have been better. Or at least more memorable. Like the Hindenburg. Or a power blackout. Yeah, years from now, people could ask, where were you on the night Andy Rally played Hamlet? Nine months later, hundreds of unexpected babies would be born. Laughing hysterically.

BARRYMORE.   Cheap vengeance, this is cheap vengeance against me. I'm sure you were ... more than acceptable. Far more.

ANDREW.   No. *(A beat.)* I've been walking all night.

BARRYMORE.   Where?

ANDREW.   Every place. The park. Fifth Avenue. All the way down to the Battery.

BARRYMORE.   All night? Were you accosted?

ANDREW.   Once. Two guys, with a knife. I just said, guys, look at me. What do you want? A farthing? A doubloon? Then they recognized me — from TV. The wrong show. I kept walking. *(The doorbell buzzes. Andrew goes to answer it.)* It's 7 AM. What is going on around here? *(Into the receiver.)* Hello? Sure. Come on up. *(To Barrymore.)* It's Gary.

BARRYMORE.   Gary? That cloud of Malibu ozone, that cultural cavity? *Night School?* Is that what you're doing?

ANDREW.   I guess we'll find out.

BARRYMORE.   Well done, Andrew! *(He toasts Andrew, with a bottle of champagne from the mantle.)* Here's to all the money you can make, and all the pride you can swallow! Here's to challenge, and risk, and *(He gestures to himself.)* the worst possible role models! Why don't you join me, Andrew, this is very good champagne! After all, you can afford it! Lucky dog! *(Andrew goes to the door. Gary enters, dressed in his usual top-of-the-line casual wear. He carriers a sheaf of newspapers.)*

GARY.   *(To Andrew.)* Hey! Hamlet! *(To Barrymore.)* Big guy! Where were you last night? You missed it! *(A beat.)* Look what I got! The papers! Or did you already see 'em?

ANDREW.   No.

GARY.   Well, let's have a look. *(Unfolding a newspaper.)* Aren't you curious?

BARRYMORE.   There is something about a person who brings the papers, with glee. Shouldn't you be hooded? *(Barrymore exits, through the archway.)*

GARY.   *(Scanning the review.)* Uh-oh ...

ANDREW.   Don't. Let me. *(Improvising.)* "A not uninteresting attempt. Far to go. If Mister Rally is to seriously consider a career on the boards, blah, blah, blah, fine supporting cast, dee dee dee, remember, it's free."

GARY.   *(Impressed.)* Not bad. You left out "TV lightweight," but that's not so terrible, huh? Coulda been worse. Personally, I thought you were terrific. Like I could tell.

ANDREW.   Gary ...

GARY.   I warned you, I said Andy, it's not for you, but hey — you learned, right? In front of all those people. Shuffling all those feet.

ANDREW.   I was there.

GARY.   I know. I know. Anyway, it's all over — back to reality. I wanted to see you, before I took off, so I can call the network. Are we on? All systems go? Start pre-production? *(Before Andrew can speak.)* Wait. I know you're gonna say yes, it's all set, but let me ... polish the party. Tickle the treat.

ANDREW.   Gary, cut it. What's the offer?

GARY.   The money. It was a feeding frenzy. The first season, 24 episodes, guaranteed — three million. That's right.

ANDREW.   Three million dollars? For one season?

GARY.   Even if it's a dud, one year and out — it's enough, to breathe, to lay back. A house. Houses. Cars. No — for your folks. For all they've done. Or, if you hate 'em, rub 'em out — the money's there. And if the show hits, okay, you're tied up for a few years, but — triple it. Quadruple. Keep going. Picture it. One day, you wake up, and whatever happens — you're rich. Something goes wrong, something breaks, it's not so bad, it's never gonna be so bad. Why? You're rich!! It's like they say, the rich are different from you and me — *(Searching for a superlative.)* they're RICH!!! *(Barrymore re-enters, and sits on the chaise, with a drink.)* On the other hand, and I'm just blowin' smoke here, pretend like you're outta your mind, pretend you say no. Pretend ... you stick around here. The theater. El footlights. And in a few years ... *(He gestures to Barrymore.)* Here you are. No offense, but — another out-of-work actor. Not so young, not so network. Maybe you wait tables. *(To Barrymore.)* Sorry — maitre'd. Pretty soon you move, 'cause you can't afford this place. But hey, once in a while — you get work. Off-off-*nowhere*. It's Chekov. It's a basement. It's July. And there's folding chairs. I'm not trying to scare you, I'm just doing my job, as a bud.

ANDREW.   Three *million* dollars?

GARY.   Plus all expenses and personal staff. Folding chairs, Andy! And you fold 'em up, after every show. AA needs the hall. Andy-boy? Are we on?

ANDREW.   Am I in? A network commitment ...

GARY.   Full season ...

ANDREW.   Three million dollars ...

GARY.   No tights.

ANDREW.   *(After a pause.)* No.

GARY.   No?

BARRYMORE.   *(Shocked.)* No?

ANDREW.   No.

GARY.   No? What, no, you still don't like the figures, no, you're not happy with the time slot?

ANDREW.   No. Just no.

GARY.   Wait. You don't get it. In LA, there is no "no." You know, like "yes" means sure, unless I get a better offer. And "no" means "yes," with more money.

ANDREW.   No. This is a New York "no." A real no. A surgical no. A final, terminal no.

GARY.   Oh. A maybe.

ANDREW.   No. Gary, it's a no like in, Gary, would you be interested in doing a documentary on acid rain for PBS?

GARY.   *(To Barrymore.)* Talk to him. Talk sense.

BARRYMORE.   *(Increasingly gleeful.)* No.

ANDREW.   No!

GARY.   Andy, you're sayin' this now, but what about tomorrow? The next day? When the bills start comin' in. When you're flyin' coach!

ANDREW.   I'm sorry.

GARY.   *(Falling to his knees.)* Andy — think about me. Think about the money I could make on this. Don't be selfish!

BARRYMORE.   *(Delighted.)* Have pity, Andrew — he's begging.

GARY.   *(To Barrymore.)* You! This is all your fault! You made him do that Hamlet crap!

BARRYMORE.   *(Innocently.)* Me? I didn't even see the play. I was home, watching television. I'm an American.

GARY.   *(Utterly bewildered.)* Jesus, what happened here? Andy, what am I going to tell the network?

ANDREW.   Tell 'em — who needs Andy Rally? Dime a dozen.

GARY.   *(Delighted.)* Yeah! That's good. That's great! Who can I get?

ANDREW.   Gary!

BARRYMORE.   *(To Gary.)* Three million dollars? *(Considering it.)* When would you need me? *(Felicia, dressed for travel in her usual gaudy fashion, pokes her head in from the front door.)*

FELICIA.   Gar?

GARY.   Babe — in the car.

FELICIA.   We're gonna miss the plane.

ANDREW.   Felicia?

FELICIA.   Hi, hon.

GARY.   Andy, I gotta make some calls. Damage control.

ANDREW.   In the kitchen. *(Gary exits, through the archway. Felicia gives Andrew a big hug.)*

FELICIA.   Hon, what can I say? Last night — were you terrific or what? I mean, the part I saw.

ANDREW.   The part you saw?

FELICIA.   Well, I caught the first act, where you were so confused. But at intermission I got thirsty, and Gary has a bar in the limo, and — Andy, I'm sorry. One thing led to another!

ANDREW.   Wait — the two of you?

BARRYMORE.   *(Tickled.)* Perfection!

FELICIA.   *(Thrilled.)* Yeah! And all thanks to you — and Shakespeare!

ANDREW.   So you only saw one act — both of you?

FELICIA.   Honey, I'm sorry. So how did it end? You're king now, right?

ANDREW.   No — Felicia, are you going away with Gary?

FELICIA.   Yeah, to LA. Long weekend. *(Admiring the apartment.)* This is a great place. I told you. I just wish we could've contacted Barrymore. But I've been thinking — you know, maybe ghosts don't really exist. Even Ma, maybe it's all in my mind. No afterlife, no other side — nothing. *(During this speech, Barrymore has crept up behind Felicia. His arms encircle her waist, from behind. He now kisses her neck passionately. She is completely oblivious.)* Who knows? *(Gary re-enters, from the archway.)*

GARY.   We gotta split. But Andy — this isn't over. I'm comin' back for you. And if I have to tie you up, drug you, and slam you into a cage — you're makin' money.

ANDREW.   Aren't you flying somewhere?

FELICIA.   We'll call you!

GARY. *(Making a phone gesture.)* From the plane, buddy. *(At the door.)* Andy, this theater thing — we'll beat it, together. *(Gary and Felicia exit. The door to the roof swings open. Deirdre appears, in a nightgown. Her hair is wild, and tangled with flowers. Her eyes are half-shut, and she rubs her upper arms. She moans; she is in a pleasure stupor. She leans against the door frame, rubbing up against it, like an extremely satisfied cat.)*

ANDREW.   Deirdre?

DEIRDRE.   Mmmm ...

ANDREW.   Deirdre?

DEIRDRE.   MMMMM ...

ANDREW.   Deirdre, are you okay?

DEIRDRE.   Mmmmmhuh ...

ANDREW.   Deirdre, I'm sorry I took off last night, after the show. I hope you went to the party. Did you ... have a good time?

DEIRDRE.   *MMM ...*

ANDREW.   Deirdre, what is going on? *(Deirdre, who has been slinking her way down the stairs, stroking the bannister, now leaps into Andrew's arms. She looks deep into his eyes and gives him a volcanic, passionate kiss.)*

DEIRDRE.   Hi.

ANDREW.   Hi.

DEIRDRE.   Mmmm ...

ANDREW.   Stop that.

DEIRDRE.   Stop what?

ANDREW.   Stop ... moaning. Deirdre, did you go to the party?

DEIRDRE.   Party?

ANDREW.   The party. After the play. We were in *Hamlet* last night, remember?

BARRYMORE.   *(Starting up the stairs.)* Perhaps I should leave you two alone.

ANDREW.   No! Stay.

DEIRDRE.   Of course I'll stay. Oh, Andrew. Last night, you were so wonderful.

ANDREW.   No, I wasn't. Deirdre, I'm not ... what you want. You're waiting for someone legendary, for a total hero, for

Lancelot, or Mark Antony. And you should. I wish I'd been good, I wish I'd been — everything. For you. And I'm sorry.

DEIRDRE. *(With real wonder.)* Andrew — I watched you on stage last night, and I thought — he has worked so hard. He's put his heart and soul into this, and at least partly for me. And he's ... so *bad.* And I thought I'd be demolished, but — something happened. I mean, people were coughing, and a plane, it just *flew* overhead, and there were all those mosquitoes.

ANDREW. Right in my mouth.

DEIRDRE. And you just kept on going! And I thought — what makes a hero? It's just someone who tries to do what's right, despite impossible odds. Like you playing Hamlet! You're the bravest, noblest man I've ever met!

ANDREW. *(Eagerly.)* Really?

DEIRDRE. Yes! But then I thought about how I'd put you off, and how I was just a lady-in-waiting, and I thought ... I'm not worthy.

ANDREW. Deirdre ...

DEIRDRE. So you know what I decided to do?

ANDREW. Something sensible?

DEIRDRE. *(Really re-living it.)* Exactly! I decided to drown myself! Like Ophelia, in Central Park Lake! Isn't that perfect? *(She runs to the chaise and stands on it.)* So I went behind the theater, and I stood on a rock and braided wildflowers into my hair! And I sang Ophelia's bawdy song ... *(Singing.)*
　　Hey nonny nonny
　　Hey nonny no ... no ...
(Desolate.) But I couldn't jump in. I lost my nerve!

ANDREW. I'm glad.

DEIRDRE. And I was so upset that I came back here and ran up to the roof! *(She tears across the stage and runs up the stairs to the landing. Barrymore is waiting; he stands right behind her. She speaks with great yearning.)* And I stood at the edge, and I gazed up at the moon! And I said, oh Mister Moon, you're so *big,* and *round,* and *yellow* ...

ANDREW. Deirdre ...

DEIRDRE. *(Very frustrated.)* I know. Please. I thought Deirdre, everyone's right. Get some help. And that's when I felt it.

ANDREW.   Felt what?

DEIRDRE.   This breeze, on the back of my neck. *(Barrymore blows gently on Deirdre's neck.)* Except it wasn't just a breeze, it was more like ... a hand. *(Barrymore lightly strokes Deirdre's neck.)*

ANDREW.   A hand?

DEIRDRE.   A caress.

ANDREW.   No. No. *(Barrymore makes a rather grand cross, moving from the staircase to the chaise, on which he stretches full out. He passes directly in front of Andrew. He is smiling, like a cross between the Mona Lisa and the Cheshire Cat.)*

DEIRDRE.   Yes! And that's all I can remember, except I woke up this morning in the room up there, and there was a rose on my pillow.

BARRYMORE.   A red rose.

ANDREW.   *(To Deirdre.)* A red rose?

DEIRDRE.   For passion. And my copy of *Romeo and Juliet* was lying open, right to one of Juliet's speeches:

> My bounty is as boundless as the sea,
> My love as deep; the more I give to thee
> The more I have, for both are infinite.

And all I could think about was you. Andrew — I'm *worthy.* *(Deirdre glides up the door to the roof. She turns to Andrew. As a sensual command.)* Get thee ... right now! *(Deirdre might also toss Andrew a rose at this point. She exits to the roof, beckoning for Andrew to follow. Andrew turns to Barrymore, absolutely furious.)*

ANDREW.   *(To Barrymore.)* I wish I could kill you! You ... you ...

BARRYMORE.   Me? She was suicidal! She felt unworthy of you!

ANDREW.   *What did you do?*

BARRYMORE.   Andrew — I'm a ghost! A spirit!

ANDREW.   A Barrymore!

BARRYMORE.   How dare you!

ANDREW.   Swear it! Nothing happened, between you and Deirdre!

BARRYMORE.   Please! You wouldn't understand! It was ... a moment of Shakespeare. A purely poetic communion, between two lyric souls, as assisted by moonlight. *(A beat.)* A midsummer night's dream.

ANDREW. *(After a beat, warily.)* Much ado about nothing?

BARRYMORE. *(Grandly, comforting him.)* As you like it.

ANDREW. So — all's well that ends well.

BARRYMORE. Indeed. Yet — I am utterly perplexed. Three million dollars. And your precious LA. Why not go?

ANDREW. Why not? Do you know what stopped me? Of all things? *Hamlet.*

BARRYMORE. But ... you were ghastly. You said so. Deirdre agreed. The papers — everyone in New York.

ANDREW. I heard. And that's part of it. Last night, right from the start, I knew I was bombing. I sounded big and phony, real thee and thou, and then I started rushing it, hi, what's new in Denmark? I just could not connect. I couldn't get ahold of it. And while I'm ... babbling, I look out, and there's this guy in the second row, a kid, like 16, obviously dragged there. And he's yawning and he's jiggling his legs and reading his program, and I just wanted to say, hey kid, I'm with you, I can't stand this either! But I couldn't do that, so I just keep feeling worse and worse, just drowning. And I thought, okay, all my questions are answered — I'm not Hamlet, I'm no actor, what am I doing here? And then I get to the soliloquy, the big job, I'm right in the headlights, and I just thought, oh Christ, the hell with it, just do it!

> To be or not to be, that is the question;
> Whether 'tis nobler in the mind to suffer
> The slings and arrows of outrageous fortune,
> Or to take arms against a sea of troubles
> and by opposing, end them.

And I kept going, I finished the speech, and I look out, and there's the kid — and he's listening. The whole audience — complete silence, total focus. And I was Hamlet. And it lasted about ten more seconds, and then I was back in Hell. And I stayed there. But for that one little bit, for that one speech — I got it. I had it. *Hamlet.* And only eight thousand lines left to go. *(The preceding monologue must grow extremely passionate; Andrew must be transported back to the previous evening onstage in the park. A lighting change and musical cues are possibilities. All of Andrew's frustrations, with his career and his life, must impact on the speech; when he reaches "To be or not to be" he should be D.C., using the audience in the theater as the audience in the park. Andrew's delivery of the soliloquy fragment should show real talent, and great emotional force. The play arcs to this moment, during which Andrew reveals the result of Barrymore's teachings; the speech should be as moving and as theatrically effective as possible.)*

BARRYMORE.   There it is! The glory of Shakespeare. *Hamlet* has changed you. Altered your course.

ANDREW.   *(Sincerely.)* Yes. And I love this apartment! Because — it's like a stage set. It's the theater. And because, once upon a time — you lived here.

BARRYMORE.   Brother Hamlet.

ANDREW.   Player King. *(They embrace.)* Stay. Teach me.

BARRYMORE.   You have already learned all that is important. You've tasted glory — now, reach skyward. Surprise everyone. *(Very solemn.)* And someday, and Andrew, this I promise you — someday you will perform ... indoors. I must go. You have a performance this evening. And ... *(He gestures to the roof.)* a matinee.

ANDREW.   Get out of here.

BARRYMORE.   I'm on my way. But I have a parting request. I was unable to witness your debut, but I must see your bow.

ANDREW.   My bow? *(Barrymore nods. Andrew, puzzled, demonstrates his bow, which is quite ordinary, a simple bend from the waist.)*

BARRYMORE.   As I suspected.

ANDREW.   What?

BARRYMORE.   It was ... perfunctory. A bow should be theater incarnate. *(Andrew gestures — "So show me." Barrymore pretends to resist, then gives in.)* Oh ... very well. Begin in a daze, still lost in the drama. *(Barrymore turns away from the audience; he might move U., and lean against the bannister of the staircase, as if utterly exhausted. He then turns toward the audience, looking dazed and spent, not sure where he is, destroyed by his own genius. Peering out.)* Good Lord — is that ... an audience? *(Barrymore hears an ovation; he spots the audience, and looks shocked and confused.*

Pointing a trembling finger at himself.) Me? *(He moves haltingly toward the footlights, as if the audience were pulling him helplessly forward.)* Into the light ... *(Barrymore stands at C., still stunned by the applause. He stretches out his arms to the orchestra section, acknowledging the love.)* All my children ... *(Barrymore crisply raises his arms to the balcony.)* And the poor! *(He gestures to either side, acknowledging the rest of the cast.)* The company ... *(He flips his hands up, dismissing the cast, and returns to self-acknowledgement.)* Don't spoil them. The finale. Your humble servant. *(A deep bow from the waist, as florid as possible. Still bent over, he lifts his head, as the ovation continues.)* Oh, stop. *(He stands erect, and crosses his hands over his heart.)* I love you all ... *(He taps his heart with his right fist, then raises the fist in a salute, with the pinky and thumb extended — this is sign language for "I love you." As he salutes.)* Especially the deaf! *(He blows a kiss, using both hands.)* And off. *(He walks backwards, his arms at his sides, his head bowed. He turns and faces Andrew.)*

ANDREW.   Virginia Smokehouse!

BARRYMORE.   On rye! Now you. *(Barrymore positions Andrew at C.; Andrew is still not quite sure what is going on.)* For the full effect ... *(Gesturing to the proscenium.)* Ring down the curtain! *(The curtain falls, then rises* immediately. *Andrew is alone onstage; Barrymore has vanished. Andrew is looking around for Barrymore, frantically. As he searches, he spots the audience. He points a trembling finger at himself — "Me?" He begins an abbreviated version of the grand Barrymore bow, acknowledging the orchestra, then the balcony, then performing the "humble servant" bend and the salute to the deaf. As Andrew salutes the deaf, a spotlight hits the chaise, illuminating the leatherbound copy of* Hamlet. *Andrew picks up the copy, and looks to heaven, as the lights on the stage dim, except for the spotlight now on Andrew. Andrew smiles.)*

CURTAIN

PROPERTY LIST

ACT ONE

Stacked groundcloths
Open box with towels
Boxes, stacked in various piles
8-foot ladder
Armor with Barrymore sword, covered
Champagne bottle (opened)
Cup of water
Empty bookcase
Vase of flowers
Crate with lamp and shade on brown paper
Sittable crate
Tall crate
Cliplight
Dropcloths
Ashtray
Hairpin
Dish towel
Andrew's sword
Telephone
Folding chair
Wrapped picture frame
Menus
Cardboard pad
Box with 2 rock glasses and candle
Champagne bottle (closed)
1/2 cigarette
Keys
Roses in vase
Barrymore book
Eyeglasses
Cigarette holder
Lighter
Cigarette case with cigarettes
Leatherbound copy of *Hamlet*
2 daggers

ACT TWO

Large pillow
3 square pillows on floor
Bookstand with book
Marble flower stand with flowers
Brass vase with pussywillows
2 books
3 pillows
2 flower arrangements
Hinged globe with glasses and red capped bottle inside
Brass stand with vase of roses
Sneakers
Draw purse
Floral arrangement
Dante bust
Urn
Rock glasses, one empty, one 1/4 full
Fancy sword
4 champagne bottles
Champagne glasses
Newspapers
Junk food wrappers

COSTUME PLOT

ANDREW RALLY

Act One, Scene 1
> Levi blue jeans
> Blue linen long-sleeve shirt
> Light-brown suede jacket
> Brown leather belt with western buckle
> New Balance tennis shoes
> Black socks

Act Two, Scene 1
> Black wool bublet with silver trim
> Beige muslin shirt with ties and spandex lower sleeves
> Black tights
> Dance belt
> Black ankle high boots

Act Two, Scene 2
> Beige muslin long sleeve shirt with ties
> Black dance belt
> Black tights
> Levi blue jean jacket
> Black socks
> Grey New Balance tennis shoes

JOHN BARRYMORE

Act One, Scene 1
> Black spandex velvet T-shaped tunic with elastic waist-
> band and three silver chains around neck
> White cotton sleeveless under garment with white
> crinkle cotton bib
> Black tights
> Black suede slippers

FELICIA DANTINE

Act One, Scene 1

Purple Spandex mini skirt
Purple print rayon blouse with knit collar and cuffs
Multi-colored beaded belt
Red print wool scarf with beaded fringe
Purple tights
Purple suede thigh-high boots
Large multi-colored bead earrings
Embroidered multi-colored pouch
Large purple shoulder bag with gold chain
Orange and purple plaid knee-length coat
Pink watch

Act Two, Scene 1

Black velvet knee-length evening gown with teal satin
    sleeves and teal satin and black net ruffle around
    hem
Black pantyhose
Black satin pumps
Large green drop earrings
Black net hair bow
Black satin clutch

Act Two, Scene 2

Donna Karen black knit unitard
Pink and black striped rayon blouse
Black suede thigh-high boots
Large pink bead earrings
Large white shoulder bag
White frame sunglasses
Fuschia scarf with pink beaded fringe
Pink and orange print scarf
Black pantyhose

LILLIAN TROY

Act One, Scene 1
> Long sleeve, black wool turtleneck shirt
> Full, mid-calf length black wool skirt
> Red print shawl (worn over right shoulder)
> 2 1/2"-wide black leather belt, with black leather buckle
> Large gold sunburst brooch (worn C.F. neck)
> Gold textured button earrings
> A.B. pear-shaped rhinestone ring
> Black full-length mink coat
> Black leather gloves
> Jet black Charter House pantyhose
> Black leather pumps
> Black slip

Act Two, Scene 1
> Black full-length evening gown with black lace bodice,
>   studed with rhinestones and a double circle black
>   silk skirt
> Silver jacquard shawl
> Jet black pantyhose
> Large rhinestone and pearl earrings
> Large rhinestone ring

GARY PETER LEFKOWITZ

Act One, Scene 1
> Beige silk pleated pants
> Beige and tan braided suede belt
> Beige silk short-sleeve shirt with yellow and blue fish
>   print
> Brown suede car coat
> Blue baseball cap
> Dark beige socks with small medalions
> Beige buckskin lace-up shoes
> Rolex

Act Two, Scene 1
>   Single-breasted tuxedo
>   Beige crew neck T-shirt
>   Fringed white silk scarf
>   Black sheer evening socks
>   Black patent leather evening pumps
>   Black leather belt

Act Two, Scene 2
>   Olive linen single-breasted suit
>   Perry Ellis Hawaiian shirt with yellow background,
>   red flowers and green foliage
>   Brown reptile-skin belt with silver western buckle
>   Dark green woven print socks
>   Olive basket weave suede lace-up shoes

DEIRDRE MCDAVEY

Act One, Scene 1
>   Orange silk mid-calf length fitted dress with scoop
>   neck and antique lace collar
>   Snap-in lace blouse and cuffs
>   Flower print pantyhose
>   Beige mesh pantyhose
>   Brown ankle-high leather boots
>   Green wool cape with hood
>   White cotton nightgown with lace collar and cuffs

Act Two, Scene 1
>   Green-and-yellow print velvet Elizabethan gown with
>   train, light green and gold brocade under skirt and
>   sleeves, and gold braid trim
>   Green and yellow knee-high socks
>   Yellow suede slippers with gold studs
>   Gold basket-weave hat with yellow flower wreath and
>   yellow chiffon drape

Act Two, Scene 2
>   Repeat of white nightgown

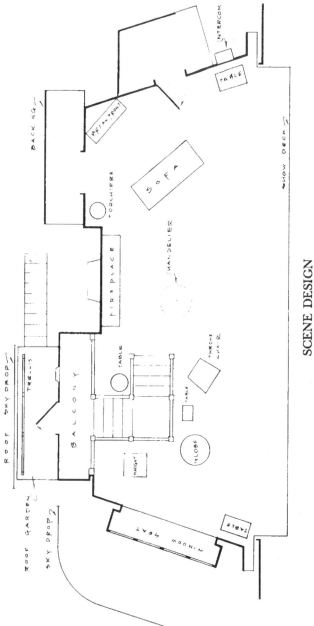

SCENE DESIGN

"I HATE HAMLET"

(Designed by Tony Straiges for the New York Broadway production)

NOTES
(Use this space to make notes for your production)

NOTES
(Use this space to make notes for your production)

NOTES

(Use this space to make notes for your production)

NOTES
(Use this space to make notes for your production)